You Have No Idea

YOU HAVE NO IDEA: Stories from the Southside

A Flamingo Press Publication

Disclaimer: You're probably not in this book. If you think you recognize yourself, it wasn't you. It was totally someone else. You may remember a similar event in which you were involved, but for sure, I didn't write about you. I promise. And I want the world to know I have nothing against the 70s, random serial killers, people who spend way too long in the bathroom, prostitutes, flamingo thieves, prison escapees, sailboats, or opossums. While I'm on the subject of animals, please know that none were harmed in the writing of this book.

All Photo Credits: Casey Hyde.

Cover design by Waxing Crescent Moon Covers

Print ISBN: 978-1-7372456-7-4

Printed in the United States of America.

❀ Created with Vellum

You Have No Idea

STORIES FROM THE SOUTHSIDE

MISSY STEINER

To Madi, my sweet angel child from heaven

Merchants on Main
M

START IN THE MIDDLE

Where to start? Please don't say the beginning. Because to be perfectly honest, there's always more than one place to start. One beginning might be too simple for its complicated end and another beginning too complicated for its simple end. One thing I know for sure—the beginning of my end or possibly the end of my beginning started with a pound on my door. A loud pound. Not a friendly knock from a neighbor there to borrow something, probably wine, and not the persistent rap of one of God's messengers there to save my soul. It was a decisive, immediate, and urgent pound. One that signaled, for better or for worse, my life would never be the same.

I held my breath, I opened the door, and there stood a man. Just a man. A man I'd never seen in my life but a man who would change it in a heartbeat when he told me he was there to evict me from my home. The home my daughter grew up in, the home we'd lived in for more than a decade, the only place either of us wanted to be at the end of the day. We were losing our home. We were losing our neighbors who had become family, our front yard, our back yard, everything in between, and the very foundation of our lives. In that one moment with that one man at my door, I lost the proverbial roof over my head. My shelter, my security, and my haven. Gone.

To be fair, he was a kind man. As odd as it sounds, the stranger on our front porch didn't like delivering the news only slightly less than I didn't like receiving it. And when he realized I had no idea it was coming, he felt just as bad as I did. It was a painful moment for both of us. I was shocked and in a state of disbelief with everything swirling around me, so I sat down before I fell down. When I asked how this could happen, he kindly and calmly explained that my home had been sold months earlier. And I was the last to know.

I had a very short amount of time to pack my daughter and my life and vacate the premises. I'm almost at a loss to describe the chaos and confusion of the following days. What to keep? What to donate? What to toss? With more than a decade of memories and possessions, the job was overwhelming. I had three floors and ten years of my life to relocate with nowhere to go.

As the news spread and numbness set in, my friends showed up. They showed up with packing boxes, tape guns, donuts, tequila, and hope. They kicked me into gear. They reminded me I was loved. I loved them back, not only with everything my heart could hold but also with everything their cars could hold. My worldly possessions were fair game. My catchphrase was "Do you like it? Do you want it? You can have it." No one who stopped by to help left without a set of sheets, a recliner, or a double-matted and framed print right off the wall. I may have even shoved a few things into their cars when they weren't looking.

One day, a friend accidentally dropped a huge box of treasures. The bottom fell out, sending slivers of porcelain and shards of glass flying. Everyone in the room stopped everything they were doing as complete silence fell. The friend who'd dropped the box, mortified, began apologizing profusely.

My daughter, barely out of high school, Sweet Angel Child from Heaven, stopped him. "It's okay," she said. "I didn't want any of it anyway. Now we don't have to move it."

The crazy laughter that followed broke the spell,

and at that moment, I realized that laughter in the face of despair would be the key to our survival.

At the time, I was a new business owner. I had a shop, a gift shop of sorts, an eclectic gathering of restored furniture, vintage housewares, and unique gifts in an up-and-coming part of town. My daughter and I would move into the small space above the store. An attic on Main Street in Chattanooga, Tennessee, would become our new home. We said goodbye to our old lives in the suburbs and hello to our new life above a store, a store that would save us in so many ways. As we left our house for the last time, never to look back, we knew that chapter of our lives was over. The final page had turned.

It was time for a new chapter, a new life, and a new adventure on the Southside. Above Merchants on Main.

And what an adventure it's been.

YOU GOTTA HAVE FRIENDS

We settled into our new lives in no small part thanks to our old friends who'd helped us get there and, surprisingly, in large part to our new friends, the amazing customers who showed up to become part of our extended family. With five thousand square feet of retail space, customers could always find something to admire, and while they were trying to decide between the green or the blue scarf, the alabaster or the brass lamp, the vanilla or the pumpkin candle, we got to know one another. There was always time for a good laugh, gossip, and catching up.

We celebrated with all our friends, old and new: their triumphs, their weddings, their engagements, and their new babies, both human and otherwise.

Some of our favorite new canine friends included a sweet Great Dane named Shorty and spunky rescue girls named Ginger and Penny. We shared the sad moments too—divorces, heartbreaks, and deaths. Often, people stopped by to see what was new, but more often, it was just to see us. Merchants on Main became the neighborhood watercooler with an old-school-beauty-parlor vibe, and we grew to love it. Regardless of how we got there, it was where we were meant to be.

Through the years, we've furnished houses, styled offices, outfitted divas and princesses, sent tourists home with fabulous keepsakes, and we've had the pleasure of wrapping thousands of gifts. Birthday gifts, wedding gifts, hostess gifts, and It's Twins! gifts. We've been blessed to meet several of the new babies and, in many cases, have had the pleasure of watching them grow up. Once, we came close to delivering a baby at the store. As it turned out, the mother was just having strong contractions, but on the Southside, you never know. Anything's possible.

This book is to honor our Southside friends, old and new. To thank them for the hope, joy, and humor they've brought to our lives. They walk in the door like a breath of fresh air to light up our days, although there are always two sides of a coin. On one side are our amazing customers. The other side… Well, that's a different story. The idea of writing all this down hit me one afternoon when one of our most memorable characters darkened our door. Trust me when I say I could never make all this up.

HOTEL

VAN MAN

It was a perfect afternoon in June. It was a Friday. Fun day. Friends day. Store traffic had slowed. My daughter left to either deliver a piece of furniture, quote a paint job, or maybe to meet friends. I don't remember exactly why I was alone, but I was, and the store was quiet. I watched the clock, waiting until I could stroll down the street to meet friends and welcome the weekend, when the bell above the door chimed, and in walked a giant.

He was an incredibly large man—a gargantuan man. He had all my attention. Starting at the top, he wore a cowboy hat of the ten-gallon variety decorated with so many feathers it was as if a peacock had landed on his head. And if that wasn't enough, below the hat, he wore a 1970s leisure suit. In sky blue. I was alone in the store with a man wearing a peacock on his head and yards upon yards upon yards of sky-blue double knit. I can honestly say I've never seen so much sky-blue double knit in one place.

Don't get me wrong. I've seen my fair share of throwback fabric. It's possible I went to a high school dance with someone wearing a suit just like it. I don't remember his name. It was the seventies. But his leisure suit was hard to forget. If you're old enough, you know exactly what a leisure suit is. If you aren't old enough, visit a vintage clothing store, and Chattanooga has a really good one just across the river. Don't forget the accessories, like Leisure Suit Man, who filled my door that Friday afternoon, who also wore a silver belt buckle the size of a salad plate. Amazingly, he had shiny silver cuffs to match the belt. The cuffs were bedazzled with jewels. Rings adorned most of his fingers. On his feet, cowboy boots the size of a professional basketball player's. He stood in the door, shining as bright as the sun.

In his leisure suit.

Under his peacock hat.

Wearing cowboy boots.

He said, "Howdy, Little Lady."

I might have waved. The ground shook as he stepped into the shop. Maybe it didn't. Maybe that was me.

He said he had a deal for me. He said he'd been cleaning his van and found something he thought I'd be interested in buying.

(Oh, really?) (I couldn't see that Leisure Suit and I had the same taste. In anything.)

In spite of the fact that this wasn't my first rodeo (people tried to sell me inventory all the time), I'm sure I said something appropriate, but maybe not, because it was then that I looked past him and saw the van he'd been cleaning. Once again, I was back in the seventies. His van was a cross between Scooby-Doo's Mystery Machine and the van from *Fast Times at Ridgemont High*. It was painted and decked out like a groovy love machine. I just knew there was a fold-down bed somewhere in the back of that van, and I could almost hear Barry White or Marvin Gaye singing in the background.

He slid a bag across the front desk to me. An old and well-worn paper bag from Ace Hardware. A small bag. One that might have originally held a handful of nails or shiny new keys. Small items. By the grace of God, I didn't stick my hand in it. Divine intervention, maybe? I did open it and peek. The first thing I saw was a rather long tail slithering up the side.

I think I jumped a foot. Maybe ten.

I closed the bag and slid it back to him, tried to smile, and held in a horror-movie scream. I might have been close to a heart attack, a stroke, or a full-body aneurysm. My voice shook when I asked, "What exactly is this, sir?"

"It's a baby alligator," he deadpanned. Straight-faced.

It was a stuffed baby alligator.

I gripped the front desk between us with white knuckles and gave him my service-industry smile. If you've ever worked in the service industry, you know the smile. I thanked him for stopping by and told him I had to pass.

"Your loss, Little Lady."

Yes.

I waited until the Love Machine cleared the parking lot, locked up the store, then batted my way down the street, stopping a few times to shake his image out of my head. Stopping a few more times to shake the baby alligator's image out of my head. I wondered what kind of Friday afternoon people who processed insurance claims were having. I wondered if there were any insurance companies hiring processors. I fell into the seat my friends had saved for me, held a finger up to the bartender, who, recognizing my deer-in-the-headlights look, poured me a double. My friends and I toasted the Van Man driving the Love Machine.

BOYS ARE TEMPORARY,
CATS ARE FOREVER

CAT LADY

I KNOW WITH ABSOLUTE CERTAINTY AND WITH EVERY fiber of my being that when my daughter and I landed on the Southside, we were given a gift. I'm still so thankful to God, the universe, and destiny. It was the perfect place for us to land. Slowly, we started to heal. Slowly, we became part of something bigger than us. Slowly, we became part of a neighborhood like no other.

We waved to people as we walked up and down the street. We smiled at one another and said good morning. There was an abundance of goodwill all around. And that goodwill was exactly what we needed to give and to receive. From the very first moment of our move, we never felt alone. We felt loved and part of a community like none we'd ever known.

Looking back, I don't know if we'd have survived a cold, hard, unwelcoming environment. The Southside was anything but. The soundtrack of our lives was the music of children playing in the park. The air we breathed was scented by baked goods and freshly ground coffee. The view from our windows was often that of strolling couples holding hands.

Love was all around. And there were always words of encouragement. "Are you okay?" weren't just empty words. When someone asked how we were, the light in their eyes that came straight from their heart let us know the sentiment was sincere. Friends and neighbors genuinely wanted to know if we were okay.

And we were.

We were okay.

We were on our way to better than okay.

The neighborhood continued to grow. New restaurants, new shops, and small businesses popped up. We thrived and succeeded as a cohesive unit on the Southside. We sent customers down the street to neighbor shops and restaurants, and they kindly returned the favors. We loved the Southside. The food, the community, and the camaraderie were then and still are the absolute best Chattanooga has to offer.

In the early years, every day brought new hills for me to climb and new challenges for me to overcome. As I walked down the stairs from my home to open the store, I'd say to myself, "I will get through this day. I will survive. I won't focus on the big picture—it's too much. I'll focus on today. I'll focus on baby steps forward."

I gravitated to positivity, spirituality, and the love for and from my daughter for courage and strength. One of my favorite positive quotes I still keep near to my heart is, "Bloom where you are planted." When I see a flower blooming and surviving in a crack in the sidewalk, I stare in awe. It's a reminder that what might seem impossible is, indeed, possible. Against all odds. Somehow, beauty and life continue to grow and thrive.

Some days were hopeless, and other days were hopelessly funny. The best days at the store were the ones filled with hugs, smiles, and belly laughs. Other days held huge surprises, almost always at the hand of seemingly normal people. (They say never judge a book by its cover, and you know what? They are correct.)

One day, an impeccably dressed woman walked into the store, perfect makeup expertly applied, every hair in place. We greeted each other, then she wandered off to browse the store. The store is much larger than it looks from the outside, and there were times when customers got lost. ("Hello?" They'd yell from a far corner. "Is anyone here? I think I'm turned around.") Since she'd been missing for long enough without saying a word, I decided to check on my customer. If for no other reason, I wanted to take another look at her makeup.

I found her with a puzzled look on her face, so I offered the standard retail inquiries. "Can I help you with anything? Are you looking for anything specific? Do you have any questions?" I always hesitate a beat before asking the last one. There were times it opened that door too wide. I never knew what they were going to ask.

"Yes," she says. "I have my eye on a cedar chest in the back."

"A wonderful piece," I said. "It's a vintage Lane in great shape."

"I'm thinking of making it into a litter box for my cat."

I might have picked up my own jaw. From the floor.

Maybe I'd misunderstood her. It happens. I've learned that when a customer tells me they're in the market for a stuffed chimpanzee or a Justin Timberlake mannequin, it's a good idea to ask them for more information, hoping they'll come back with something normal. ("I meant a charcuterie cookbook." Or from her, maybe, "I'm looking for vintage Chanel.") I said, "Excuse me. *What?*"

She repeated herself, word for word. "I'm thinking of making it into a litter box for my cat."

Nope. I heard her right the first time. She wanted to cut out the side of a vintage Lane cedar chest and turn it into a master bath for a cat.

"Wow," I said. "That's really... thinking out of the box."

(She didn't get it.)

"Don't you think it would work?" she asked.

Oh, I had so many thoughts. So many questions. One was "Who in their right mind would spend three hundred dollars on a litter box for their cat?" Was her cat a two-hundred-pound tiger? Was I being filmed for an episode of *Punk'd*? Was someone about to say, "Smile. You're on *Candid Camera!*" Were the guys from *Impractical Jokers* hiding somewhere?

"I'm not sure," I said, scrambling for words to discourage her, "but I've heard some pets are allergic to cedar."

"Why would that matter?" she shot back, almost offended, as if I were the one being ridiculous.

"Well, it's a cedar chest. Made of cedar. If your cat's allergic to cedar..."

You can explain it all you want, but you can't understand it for them.

"I'm going home to think about it," she said.

(If I had a nickel for every time I've heard that line...)

I pasted on my service industry smile. "If you decide you want the chest, give me a call," I said. "I'll be happy to hold it for your cat."

I knew I'd never hear from her again.

And I was okay with that.

I saw her out and locked up, another day conquered. It had been a profitable and fun day filled with friends stopping by, and with Cat Lady bringing up the rear, another day of unexpected hilarity. That day, as the neighborhood strolled down the street to clink glasses and swap stories, we toasted her.

Meow.

WHITE MOUNTAIN
I HAD ONE OF THOSE!
BINGO
1000 PIECE PUZZLE

BINGO

I DON'T REMEMBER EXACTLY WHEN WE STARTED playing bingo at the store. Years ago. It's still such a fun game to play while also surprisingly challenging. Some days, lining up the squares for a win wasn't unlike the planets aligning. It was rare. My friends and I adapted our version of Shop Bingo from a very funny game called Walmart Bingo. You know the one —a square filled for someone with a mullet, someone in pajamas, a whole family riding in a shopping cart, someone in a swimsuit or maybe even their underwear. When it comes to Walmart shoppers, the possibilities are endless. We took that game and made it our own.

Shop Bingo starts with two easy squares. One, when a customer asks about the stairs (happens all the time), and another dedicated to the paint-spackled version of Sweet Angel Child from Heaven, which also happens all the time. My beautiful daughter is always splattered in paint. It's on her clothes, on her face, and even in her hair. The first two squares are almost gimmes, like free spaces. Harder squares to fill include a customer asking for an impossible item, like a carburetor for a Ford Mustang, a pink toilet, or anything signed by Pope Francis. Two other squares are filled if one of our neighborhood bartenders stops by or if someone we met in one of our neighborhood bars visits. We call those squares One of Our Bartenders Stopped By and Someone We Met in a Bar Stopped By. Because we're clever like that.

There's also a square for every retail worker's least favorite customer joke that isn't funny the first time, much less the one millionth time, "If it doesn't have a price on it, it must be free!" I always want to say, "Lady, you aren't nearly as funny as you think you are, and I'm trying to make a living here." But what I do is fake laugh along with them and say, "Sorry! That was yesterday!"

Another customer habit, one that maybe should be a Shop Bingo square, is shoppers stopping to read aloud whatever they find in writing, like a plaque that says, "When I get tired of shopping, I sit down and try on shoes." Or a kitchen towel that says, "You people must be exhausted from watching me do everything." The acoustics of our store being what they are, which is you-can-hear-a-gnat-sneeze, we always know exactly where the customers are. And when they're reading tea towels, we know they're not too far from more... delicately worded... items. An innocent example would be a card that says, "Shut up, Liver. You're fine." Or "I like my men like I like my coffee." (It gets a little snarkier, shadier, and a lot more sarcastic.)

Our read-aloud customers pause at the adult readables. It goes one of two ways. Either they laugh like crazy and stay there forever, or there's total offended silence. Followed by sharp footfalls. They stomp out but not before giving me a church-lady glare. Some are even Google proficient and tell the world to watch out for the Sin Section. (Really?) But I'm not bitter. Really, I'm not.

New square. Church Lady.

A surprisingly easy square to fill is dedicated to math. After ringing up a customer and giving them the total for their purchase, more often than you'd imagine, they pause. Clearly, they think something's not right. Together, we go over the items and the prices. There are a few moments of silent calculation then oral consultation with a friend who might be better at complicated math problems, until finally, it dawns on them. "The tax!" Then they look at me. "You charge sales tax?" Well, yes. As a matter of fact, I do. It's the law.

One square is We Weren't Sure You Were Open. I've asked around. This happens to other businesses as well. It's not to be understood or explained. It's a mystery of the universe. Cars are in the parking lot, lights blaze throughout the store, and OPEN signs are on both doors. We have a chalkboard sign that says, "Come in! We're open!" We even have a sparkly flashing light declaring our openness. Should we hire a flippy-sign guy to stand on the sidewalk? I have no idea where all the confusion comes from, but it happens so often we have a bingo square for it.

Three squares are dedicated to shoppers' bathroom habits. There's Flushes More Than Once, Don't Go in There, and Bathroom Hog for when we're at the front desk staring at the bathroom door and wondering if the customer has decided to move in. (Keep reading for an entire chapter dedicated to the bathroom.)

We had one guy who came in so often we started an Excel spreadsheet on him to track his bathroom habits. (Because in addition to everything else, we love statistics.) His longest bathroom visit was forty-five minutes. (That had to be a nap.) (Bathing in our sink?) (Maybe he was touching up his highlights. In our bathroom. And the small garbage can would be full of little square foils.) (Should we call 911? *What if he died in our bathroom?)* We played Rock Paper Scissors to decide who would check on him, and somewhere near round five hundred eleven, the bathroom door finally cracked. Afterward, I zipped up my hazmat suit, grabbed the ten-gallon drum of Clorox, fired up the pressure washer, and went in. Such is the life of a business owner.

Honestly, I think more shops need bingo games.

Does anyone know how I can get a patent on my Shop Bingo game? What if it catches on, and I expand with Restaurant Bingo? If I'm successful, you'll have me to thank the next time you darken a restaurant door, ask for a lemon cut into sixteen wedges, no seeds, served on a white saucer, please, and the waiter whips out his Restaurant Bingo card and marks off a square.

The trick is to find something that makes you smile on the bad days. Laughter is mine. And Shop Bingo is so very funny. Maybe it's me. Maybe I'm a crazy magnet. Crazy is attracted to me. And I have a bingo game to prove it.

MUSHROOM
MUSHROOM
MUSHROOM
CARE COVER

CLIMBING THE STAIRCASE TO NOWHERE

It's hard to explain the fascination with our staircase.

We've been here ten years. Before that, the building was empty. For forever. A good friend bought the building at a public auction. We came up with the idea for Merchants on Main and went to work. It took months to clean everything, and that took too many overflowing dumpsters to count. Judging by the bulk of what was hauled off, I think the last occupants might have been carpet-industry adjacent. Before that, I've heard many Southside neighborhood buildings were bars, which I believe because we have a room that still has No Minors Allowed painted on the wall. Rumor has it our building was once a grocery store. Rumor also has it our building was once a brothel. The only thing I know for certain is our building has always had a staircase.

The staircase snakes up the wall to the left of the desk at the front of the store, so there's no missing it. It's a metal spiral number with thin dusty memories of long-ago carpet on the rickety steps—not much to look at—but to hear our customers tell it, you'd think we had the Eighth Wonder of the World. Built and installed decades before pesky building and safety codes were a thing, the flimsy balusters beneath the skinny handrail are far enough away from one another that a small adult could walk—or fall—straight through. No one in their right mind would let a child anywhere near the spiral stairs of death.

The morbid curiosity with the staircase comes not only from its relic properties but also because it goes absolutely nowhere. Like I said, we've been here ten years. It's not like we designed, asked for, or approved of the crazy staircase. We inherited it. When we moved in, the stairs led to second-floor offices. We closed them off for fear of death by staircase. The steps were nearly impossible to navigate, they were a tragedy waiting to happen, and when I tried to carry so much as a paperclip while climbing up or careening down, I could feel the Grim Reaper breathing down my neck. We said no more death-trap stairs, closed them off, then added a set of stairs leading to the second floor. You know, normal stairs.

Why the fascination? I wish I knew. Customers step in the door, stop, and stare. Then the questions start. Next, the line. (The same line, every time.) "Look. It's the stairway to nowhere." Always—*always* —followed by laughter. (It's never me laughing. It's the stair-curious customer who laughs at their own perceived-original line.) I wish I'd started on day one and kept count of how many times someone sang me a line from "Stairway to Heaven." I've spent way too much time wondering if our staircase was actually the inspiration for the song. Does anyone remember ever seeing Led Zeppelin on the Southside?

Nine times out of ten, the staircase-curious ask if it's for sale. I want to ask back, "Why? What in the world would you do with it?" Instead, over and over again, I say, "Sorry, but no. The staircase is attached to the ceiling and the floor." (Which was obvious.) But what I want to say is, "What about a wall? Are you interested in a wall? We have several. Pick one out, and we'll knock it down for you. How about a roof? Are you in the market for a roof?"

Often, these staircase conversations happen while I'm in the middle of nine other things. I might be giving directions to one customer, answering another customer's question, ringing up a third customer, all while answering the phones and wrapping a gift. Still, the staircase-curious person hounds me with questions. "Do you know what color the carpet on the steps used to be?"

No. I did not.

Eventually, they run out of questions. Which is when they start taking selfies. In front of the staircase.

Go figure.

I try to always find a good quote. When it comes to our amazing staircase, I like this one by Lemony Snicket. "What might seem to be a series of unfortunate events may, in fact, be the first steps of an amazing journey."

SWEET ANGEL CHILD FROM HEAVEN'S SIDE OF THE STORY

HELLO FROM DEEP INSIDE THE PAINT BOOTH. MY NAME is Madeline, Madi to most. I'm Missy's daughter, her Angel Child from Heaven (humiliating), the Merchants on Main Wynonna to her Naomi, the cheese to her mac, the Stitch to her Lilo, the one who always has paint in her hair. While Mom's store world is the front desk (gossiping with her friends, customers, total strangers, the Dominos delivery guy, the UPS man, the mailman, and on quiet days, she'll gossip with the wall), my store world is the paint booth. For one, I like my own company. For two, I listen to good podcasts while I'm painting. For three, I take something old and battered and give it a new lease on life. It's my gift. And it isn't always easy.

Most of my clients are Google, YouTube, and

Pinterest pros. They like to think they know more about my work—work I've spent years perfecting—than I do. Diligently studying paint and restoration techniques has made me the painter I am today. Some days, it's all I can do not to come unglued when a customer says, "Joanna Gaines says you're supposed to use primer. Do you use primer?"

I smile.

That's all.

I smile.

As someone who does custom work for clients to their specifications, I get some pretty interesting requests, and as someone who does all that painting in the store, sometimes I have a pretty interesting audience.

One day, I was focused on painting a dresser for a client who was very particular. With-a-fine-tooth-comb particular. I've worked with her for years, often painting the same piece over and over again, just about every time a new issue of *Architectural Digest* hit the stands. Trends changed, and she changed with them. As I was painting in my studio, a tall lady with blue cotton candy for hair stopped and stared. Hard. She examined me and studied my every move. I kept working.

Fifteen minutes later, I gave up. I asked, "Can I help you?"

Instant regret.

"What to this you do?" she asked in a very thick Russian accent. Like Cartoon Natasha. Hoping I was answering whatever question she'd asked, I said, "I'm a custom painter, and I'm painting this piece for a client."

"I no like it," she said.

"Well, it's what the customer wants."

"I talk to you about paint."

(Oh, lady, please don't.)

"I paint twenty years."

(Huge internal eyeroll.) (Small external smile.) "Yay, you." At which point, I put my brush down, I stood up, and I waited to hear her tell me how to do my job.

She points. "Open to the paint."

"Open the paint?"

"You not hear too good?"

It was high school all over again.

I opened the can of blue paint I'd just closed. As I opened it, I bragged on it, because I liked to babble about paint when someone was on my last nerve. "We use a specific chemical formula of paint I find superior to other paints."

"We to see." Then she reached over and *stuck her finger in the paint,* and if that wasn't enough, *she sniffed her finger*. Blue hair tipped back, she all but put the paint finger up her nose.

Mom and I have often talked about a safe word we can yell or text to each other at times like these. We need to do that. (*"Cornbread!" "Pistachio ice cream!" "Bueller!"*) If we'd had one, I'd have used it then. Because the lady had paint on her nose.

Should I tell her?

Should I reach over and wipe it off?

Should I pray to God the fire alarm goes off right then and there?

"You to clean this piece before paint? What on it before you paint? The bubble gums? The red wines? You leave this piece to rain outside?" She didn't let me answer before she said, "You make distress this piece too much. Why you to do that?"

I must admit her disapproval was easier to take with paint on her nose.

"Again, ma'am, it's a custom piece. I'm restoring it to the client's specifications. This is how the customer wants it."

"Customer stupid."

(The nerve.)

While giving me a death stare over my alleged mismanagement of the piece, she *stuck her finger back in my paint*, going for round two. She gave me a final disapproving grunt, turned, and walked out. With blue paint on her nose.

I called it a day and went down the street to our neighborhood Cheers. I ordered a whiskey and Coke.

Bonus Paint Thoughts from Mom

At one time, we carried a boutique line of paint for the DIYer that was so well packaged it demanded attention. Our customers couldn't resist the small jar with the cute label, cute name, and cute little transparent window showing the really cute paint color. Clearly marked: paint.

You wouldn't believe the customers who opened it to smell it. As if the paint had candle properties too. As if Marchberry might actually smell like March. And berries. Without fail, the customers came away with Apricot Milkshake on their nose or Straw That Broke the Camel's Back all over their white sweater.

The closest a paint-splattered customer ever came to explaining it was this: "I saw the label. I read the label. It clearly said paint, but my brain kept saying candle." (She'd tipped over Toasted Salmon, a really pretty color that did look like a pink on its way to gray, and lucky for her, it *was* paint and not a scented candle.)

If you come to the store, ask to see where the designer paint display was. The paint palette you'll see on the concrete floor from all the mistaken sniffs tells the history of the colors we've carried through the years.

Did Angel Child from Heaven get her artistic talent from me? Probably not. In all these years, I've picked up a paint brush exactly once just to touch up a spot I thought she'd missed. (She knew all about it.) (According to her, I'd jumped the gun. Again.) (I was just trying to help.) The piece was black, but I picked up a brush with white paint hiding deep in the bristles. Now I'm not allowed to touch the paint brushes.

Danny Kaye said, "Life is a great big canvas. Throw all the paint on it you can."

Words we live by on the Southside.

BIKE GUY

CHRISTMAS IN RETAIL, CHRISTMAS IN RETAIL, SOMEONE please save me from Christmas in retail. It's the best, and it's the worst. I have two Christmas retail requests. One, please don't leave your children unattended. Two, find a way to work a retail shift during the holidays. I promise you'll learn a lot, and it might change your life. It will certainly change your shopping perspective to one of peace, goodwill, and God bless us, every one of us, especially everyone in retail.

Some of my favorite customers to wrap holiday gifts for are the big kids—some might say young adults—who have no idea we wrap gifts. "For real? You'll do that? OMG, thank you!" And in almost every case, I gained a customer for life. I wonder how many of them think I invented the concept of holiday gift wrapping. And that my idea is catching on at the mall.

My heart melts when children (attended children) choose a Christmas gift for their mom or dad. So many times, it's the first time they've purchased a gift. They're serious, they're focused, they're funny, they're adorable, and they've told me things I'll take to my grave. "What do your mommy and daddy like to do?" can be a very loaded question because eight-year-olds don't have filters.

Older, or I should say adult holiday shoppers often struggle to find gifts too. Everyone's busy around the holidays, and many shoppers come to me completely unprepared. "I have seven sisters-in-law. I only like two of them. But I still need seven sister-in-law gifts exactly the same, except I want two of them to be nicer than the other five. But still the same." I try my best. When I present them with seven perfect wrapped gifts, two secretly marked for the sisters-in-law my shopper actually likes, it's ho, ho, ho all the way around.

In the old days, in my old life, I decorated every room in my home. I hung mistletoe everywhere. I faithfully sent more than a hundred Christmas cards every year. My holiday party calendar was booked solid. Every year, I hosted a Christmas brunch for twenty at our house, complete with Christmas china, the good crystal, the good linens, pine-scented soap in the guest baths, and Bing Crosby in the background.

Our first Christmas upstairs on the Southside was like Christmas on another planet. Nothing was the same or even recognizable. But I'm the mom. And I felt like I should decorate. So I asked Sweet Angel Child from Heaven, "What do you think? Should we put up a tree? Hang stockings?"

She gave me the blankest of looks. "Mom. Have you been downstairs? If I want to see Christmas, I'll just walk downstairs."

She had a good point. We'd decked the halls in the store. There were Christmas trees everywhere. We had Santa. We had reindeers. We had elves. We had gifts, we had garland, and on everything, we had glitter. Glitter reigned supreme. Downstairs? Christmas Central. Upstairs? Peace on Earth. Not a speck of glitter in sight.

As Christmas nears, the pace of the store changes. Panic sets in, and we go into gift-wrap-overdrive mode. The phone rings with customers looking for the perfect gift. Christmas flies in the door from our vendors. Merchandise arrives by the truckload. Dealers bring in more items than you could imagine would fit in their cars. Like clowns spilling out of clown cars, Christmas keeps coming from their trunks.

Once, in the middle of all this holiday-unloading cheer, I noticed a guy in the parking lot, riding his bike in circles. Round and round he went, with his gray ponytail flying behind him. It was a chopper-looking bicycle. You know the kind—handlebars up to next week, frame stretched out to next month, and low to the ground, really low to the ground. He was almost on the ground. Seemingly bored with the parking lot, he decided to ride his chopper into the store. Yep, just rode his bike through the door.

He parked in the middle of the entrance.

Everything stopped.

No one took a breath.

Everyone turned to me. Waiting. Waiting for me to do something. (Like, WHAT?)

"Sir?" I don't think I'd blinked yet. "Can I help you?"

Remember, he's blocking the entrance—and the exit—with his Easy Rider. No one could come or go. And by no one, I mean a dozen paralyzed women.

Easy Rider: "Yeah. I'm looking for six-foot sections of bubble wrap."

(Just when I thought I'd heard it all.)

Me: "We don't sell bubble wrap, but I'd be happy to give you some. I don't know about six-foot sections, but I'll give you every single inch of bubble wrap I have if you'll leave."

(I didn't really say that last part.)

Remember, it was Christmas. And not only are dealers trying to move large boxes of inventory in, but holiday shoppers also want in. I held up a wait-a-minute finger to Easy Rider, raced for my bubble wrap stash, and gave him every scrap. He took each section and examined it. Judged size and quality. Dropped sections that didn't meet his bar to the floor. Then as quickly as he came, he left for parts unknown. With his bubble wrap.

No one moved a muscle. It was a moment frozen in time. Finally, we looked at one another. Did that just happen? Was he real? Was he the ghost of Christmas Never? On a chopper bike? Did we imagine him? Nope, we saw him, and there was bubble wrap strewn on the floor to prove it. We watched him circle the parking lot one final time, bubble wrap and ponytail flapping in the wind. We'd survived another encounter of the store unexplainable.

The holidays can be stressful, especially when they change because of death, illness, divorce, financial hardships, or any other number of reasons. If your Christmas changes, and if you feel lost, the best advice I can give is for you to change with it. Create your own happy holiday. Do something completely different. It might not feel right at first, but don't give up.

You have the rare opportunity to break away from traditions, like strawberry pretzel salad, which really makes no sense—a salad with strawberries and pretzels—and make the holidays anything you want them to be. It's your holiday. Friendsgiving? (Something we love!) Do it at Christmas. Have a potluck dinner and eat on paper plates with the amazing people in your life.

Remember my old Christmas brunch with the good linens? Our new Christmas brunch is at Waffle House. Scattered, smothered, and covered with love, for which I am so thankful. With a long list of perfect Christmases past, I can honestly say I've never been happier at the holidays than I am today.

Lastly, generously tip your servers during the holidays. Be nice to the lady ringing you up at the grocery store. Be patient with the customer service person at Macy's who absolutely did not lose your package. She's just trying to help. *Be a little kinder to the people around you.* And in closing, the blessings of peace, the beauty of hope, the spirit of love, the comfort of faith, may these be your gifts this holiday season.

Oops,
I'm
drunk.

TRIFECTA CUSTOMER DAY

THEY SAY THINGS COME IN THREES: THREE FRENCH hens, three blind mice, and three sheets to the wind. On the Southside, we enjoy the occasional three-ring circus. It happens so often in January. Why? I don't know. But in the calm after the Christmas storm, I never see it coming.

One thing I love about January is it's slow at the store. I take a deep breath. The days are filled with holiday cleanup, which is to say glitter removal, and by that, I mean mission impossible.

The peace that settles after Santa comes and goes lulls me into thinking the crazies have cleared out. Moved on. But as soon as I let my guard down, I'm proven wrong. I'll never understand how it works. The universe, maybe? Something kicks in, and the bizarre return to the Southside. And maybe because the stage of January is so quiet, when the wacky returns, it's deafening.

Enter Crazy Customer One, a man who wants to sell me an antique camera.

Me: "Thanks for thinking of me, but I don't buy antiques."

Crazy Customer One: "Yes, you do."

Me: "No, sir, I don't."

Crazy Customer One: "I heard you did. Someone sent me here because you buy antiques. He knows someone who sells all his antiques to you."

(Not true. Couldn't be. Because like I said, I don't buy antiques.)

"Let me speak to The Guy," he said. "The Boss Man."

Me: "I am The Guy. I am the Boss Man."

Crazy Customer One: "No, you're not."

We were getting nowhere, and there was nowhere to go, so I sent him down the street. I fired up my industrial leaf blower and went back to work on the glitter stuck to the ceiling. Half an hour later, Crazy Customer Two walked through the door. She was obviously in a chemically altered state, or maybe her eyes were naturally that bloodshot, her head jerked like that all the time, and she always talked all over herself. Things were about to get more interesting.

The following happened in the span of five minutes. Maybe less. No kidding.

Crazy Customer Two, aka Crazy Hot Mess: "Did a man come in here and try selling you a camera?"

Me, a little hesitantly: "Yes. But I don't buy antiques. I sent him down the street."

Crazy Hot Mess: "OMG. How long ago?"

Me: "Maybe thirty minutes?"

Now, here was where things got even more interesting.

Crazy Hot Mess: "He stole all my clothes."

(I'd been wondering.)

Crazy Hot Mess: "He stole my clothes, my money, and my camera."

Me: "Why would he do that?"

Crazy Hot Mess: "Because he's my baby daddy."

Oh, then I understood. (I did *not* understand.) But that's exactly what she said.

She went on to tell me they were in the process of opening a business, or she might have said he and his wife (plot twist) were trying to open a business, but I don't speak drug, so it was hard to know. My take-away was that someone somewhere somehow was trying to open a business, and what that had to do with me, I had no idea. At the end of her story, she slammed her head down on the front counter. I knew she was still alive because she started praying. Lord, get her out of the parking lot. Sweet Jesus, send someone to pick her up. God in Heaven, let her baby daddy come back. Almighty, let someone answer the phone.

I didn't know if I should join in ("Amen, Sweet Jesus"), anoint her with glitter, or dial 911. It was over as fast as it started. She raised her head and said, "I'm going to buy a house for my niece."

I should have called 911.

I, trying hard to think of an appropriate response to her announcement, wondered if I should respond at all, on the edge of annoyed that I was even in a situation where I had very little choice but to respond. "Wonderful. Buying a house is a lot of work. I'm sure you need to be there." *(Or anywhere but here.) (Please.)* That was when she dragged out a set of keys on a Mercedes keyring and slapped them down. (Baby Daddy had been driving an old pickup truck.)

Crazy Hot Mess went on to tell me her daughter was getting married and planned to wear a medieval princess bridal gown. There was more, way more. I caught mailbox, enchiladas, and something about a botanical garden. Let's remember that half an hour earlier, I'd been minding my own business. Rounding up glitter.

Crazy Hot Mess was in the middle of something

about unicycles when I jumped in, last resort before 911. "Can I call someone for you?"

She took me up on it, or more accurately, she took my phone. She dialed random numbers, and not surprisingly, no one answered.

Lo and behold, enter Crazy Customer Three. Crazy Hot Mess was dialing away while I worried for my phone's safety when a blue pickup truck pulled up to the side door, and I mean literally Up. To. The. Door. Another foot, and he'd have been inside. He walked in with an old lantern with no base, cracked glass, covered in blood. It could have been rust, but I'm going with blood. Crazy Hot Mess eyed him up and down, and I just looked up. To the heavens.

I said, "Really? Another one?"

Crazy Customer Three wound up for his pitch. I stopped him before he could start. "I don't buy antiques."

Crazy Customer Three said, "The guy down the street said you did. He sent me to you."

The guy down the street who kept sending people to me had better watch out if I ever found him.

Crazy Customer Three shook his lantern. The broken glass rattled. "If you won't buy it, who will?"

I couldn't send him where I'd sent Crazy Customer One with the camera not half an hour earlier, or I'd lose a Southside friend, so I said, "I have no idea."

Guess what happened next. Just guess.

Crazy Hot Mess gave Crazy Customer Three several options: have a yard sale in my parking lot (she was sure I wouldn't mind), set up a booth at a flea market (she was sure I could make that happen), or sell it on eBay (she was sure I'd let him use my computer). (Nope. None of that was happening.) "How about the Boulevard?" he asked her. "I hear they buy antiques."

Crazy Hot Mess, shocked, reeling in disbelief, says, "Are you out of your mind? *Never* go to the Boulevard." She launched into a story about a girl fight she'd been in with a lunatic biatch—Crazy Hot Mess was not the victor—on the Boulevard. All that as if there were a direct connection between his selling a worthless lantern in the vicinity of where she'd lost a fight.

First of all, the Boulevard covers miles and miles.

Second of all, Crazy Hot Mess was calling another woman a lunatic biatch.

Third of all, I didn't ask for *any* of this.

And fourth of all, Crazy Customer Three's blue pickup was blocking my door. At the very least, it was a fire hazard. If I asked him to move it, maybe he'd leave. Even better, if I asked him to give Crazy Hot

Mess a ride to her baby daddy or her medieval daughter's place or the home she was maybe buying for her niece, I could kill two birds with one stone.

It worked. They sailed off into the sunset like the perfect ending of a Hallmark movie, and I moved on with my life. Until my phone started blowing up with strangers returning Crazy Hot Mess's calls. I answered the first call, ignored the second, blocked the third, and was on my way to the back door to toss the phone as far as I could throw it when Sweet Angel Child from Heaven returned from a furniture delivery.

I grabbed my purse and dropped my ringing phone in it. "I have an appointment. Good luck. I love you."

"Good luck?" She watched me leave.

My appointment was with a bottle of wine down the street.

THINGS OVERHEARD IN THE STORE

WE'VE HEARD IT ALL.

It's amazing what we've overheard at the store through the years. People say things with us standing right there, as if we're invisible. What is it about a cash register that makes people overshare? Bartenders hear it all the time, and so do hair stylists. There's something about the snap of the plastic cape around the neck—like a truth noose in a salon chair—that says to clients, "Time to spill the beans."

It happens in retail too. We're constantly on the receiving end of unfiltered commentary. I choose to consider these snippets little gifts. Gifts that sometime teach us life lessons.

One day, two ladies were studying a display of gorgeous pottery.

Lady Number One: "Why is this coffee mug so expensive?"

Me: "Well, quality hand-made pottery is very labor-intensive."

Lady Number Two to Lady Number One: "We should make our own pottery."

Me (to myself): Great idea. Stop everything you're doing. Find a teaching studio and take expensive classes for at least a year. Buy yourself a potter's wheel, a table, lots of splash pans, a kiln, and a truck-load of supplies. Tear up your family room, kitchen, or garage. At the end of two years, you'll be broke, every stitch of clothing you own will be ruined, your back will hurt all day, every day, but you'll have a coffee mug that looks like a six-year-old made it in art class at elementary school. Or you could pay $28.95 for the artisan mug you think is too expensive.

We carry a line of custom wood signs that often get the same reaction. A lady holds up a sign to her friend and says, "This is expensive. We could make this. It would be so easy."

What I don't say is "Sure. Go to Ace Hardware. Have wood cut to size. Unless you already have a table saw. And chisels. And probably a circular saw. And know how to use all those tools. You'll need a planer, too, unless you don't mind a rough and splintered finish. And stain. And paint. Oh, and stencils but only after you design the sign. You are a graphic designer, right? Or you could pay fifty-five dollars for the gorgeous sign you're holding."

I know I sound sarcastic—guilty—but I hear it too much. And maybe to me, who often knows the person behind the art, comments like those devalue the talent, investment, and hard work of the artist just trying to make a living. What I really want to say to customers who think it all looks so easy is "You could make it yourself, but are you willing to go through all that? Can you afford to go through all that? Stay in your lane, lady, and support the artist who did all the work for you. Life is short. Buy the mug."

My least favorite fly-on-the-wall or shop-owner-behind-the-register scenario falls under the general heading of Be Kind. Or maybe Choose Your Friends Wisely. It happens often too. One friend chooses a dress, a top, pants, or another article of clothing. She slips away to try it on. She comes out beaming. Twirling. "Don't you love it?"

Her friend responds with a critical eye. A contemplative chin tap. An "I don't know..." then proceeds to talk her out of it.

(I'm behind the register, rolling my eyes so hard they're almost in the back of my head.)

"You know? The color. It makes your skin look grellow."

"Grellow?"

"Not gray, not yellow, but grellow. And it makes your shoulders look... I don't know... linebackery."

"Linebackery?"

"Like a linebacker's."

I'm behind the register, sitting on my hands so I won't jump the desk and strangle the critical friend.

"Don't do it," the critical friend says. "You'll hate yourself."

At which point, the friend who looks perfectly lovely in the new dress, top, or pants already hates herself. She's been beaten down in front of an audience. Me. And I've just about come unglued. That's when the defeated friend slinks away to change back into her old clothes.

The critical friend always, always, always turns to me to explain. Takes me into her confidence. Gives me a red-carpet commentary on the depth of her friend's bad taste. And the whole time, she's wearing a T-shirt featuring bedazzled bars of soap that says, "Wash your hands and say your prayers because Jesus and germs are everywhere." That's *her* style. She chose it, pulled it over her head, and walked out the door wearing it.

Women, listen to me. Build your friends up. Don't rip them to shreds with your judgment when you're in no position to judge. (I think Jesus said that.)

Overheard conversations aren't all critical. Sometimes we overhear the absurd.

Along with everything else under the sun, we carry novelty items. Truly, there's something in the store for everyone. Now, why there's a market for a framed photograph featuring a fleet of alien spaceships flying over Chattanooga, blowing up one of our historic bridges, I do not know. But we sold a ton of them. It was a love-hate photo. There wasn't much ambivalence. Customers into *Star Wars* and *Battlestar Galactica* loved it.

Other-side-of-that-coin customers would stare at it for too long then ask me, "What is the point of this?"

I would answer, "It's supposed to be funny."

To which they'd usually say, "It's not."

Once, I'm not kidding, a customer, shaking the photograph, said, "Did this really happen?" She was serious. She seriously asked me if there'd been an alien invasion of Chattanooga, and she was just now hearing about it at Merchants on Main.

Sidenote: there's a really good chance she drove over the very bridge annihilated in the picture to get to the store.

Sometimes we hear things that are not suitable for children.

One day, two dignified women were in the store.

They shopped. They made their way to the register with their selections. They were well dressed, had perfect hair and fresh manicures, and looked very much like they were on their way to high tea. I guess they couldn't see us standing there ringing up and wrapping their purchases, because they didn't push the pause button on the conversation they were in the middle of.

Lady Number One: "He is a nice guy, but I think he's a pervert."

Lady Number Two: "Why would you think that?"

Lady Number One: "Did you not hear about him breaking his penis?"

Merchants on Main Employees: Collective gasps. Antennae all the way up. Recording microphones on smart phones engaged.

Lady Number Two: "*No!*"

Lady Number One: "Yes. He broke his penis."

Lady Number Two: "*How?*"

Merchants on Main Employees: *Yes, how?*

Lady Number One uses air quotes. "I heard he was having 'relations' with a 'large' girl. She was very 'enthusiastic,' and now his penis is broken."

Lady Number Two: "I've never heard of such. How does one treat a broken penis? It's not like they can put a cast on a penis, can they? Is there such a thing as a penis sling? Do you think it's like a broken toe? Are they treating it with splints? How would his clothes fit over the splints on his penis? I've always thought of penises as more pliable than that." She grabs her friend's arm. "Was there a *bone* in his penis?"

And with that, the overheard-at-the-store bar was raised through the roof.

We spent the rest of the afternoon replaying the conversation. It was an entirely new level of trash talk we never saw coming. Straight to the gutter, we went. Afraid of leaving cyber tracks on our store computer, we decided not to ask Dr. Google about broken-penis causes, symptoms, and treatment. Can you imagine the erectile dysfunction advertisements we'd have to delete for years to come? And since we'd already heard what could never be unheard, we didn't want to see what could never be unseen.

"Listen and learn" is good advice I've heard all my life. In retail, sometimes it's "Listen and don't sleep for days." Broken Penis Day was one of those times, one for the books, and that afternoon, we celebrated it with wild abandon.

SOUTHERN STYLE
hash browns

RANDOM QUESTIONS

STEPPING INSIDE THE MERCHANTS ON MAIN'S DOOR, you're greeted with vibrant colors, inviting aromas, good vibes, home décor and personal treasures on every available surface, and a warm welcome from a friendly face. Why anyone would wade through all that adorable and ask for car parts is beyond me.

"Hmmm." I surveyed my surroundings, hoping the man asking would do the same. "No car parts. Sorry."

"Do you know where they do sell car parts?"

"Maybe AutoZone?"

"Where is AutoZone?"

"Maybe ask Siri? I don't know where the closest AutoZone is."

He was a little irritated. At me. "Thanks a lot, lady." He stomped out.

Sadly, he wasn't the first to walk into my shop full of ladder-back kitchen chairs and every-single-shade-of-blue cashmere wraps and ask for car parts. He won't be the last. I don't understand and can't explain the constant quest for car parts.

Second place goes to appliances.

"Do you carry washers and dryers?"

I was arranging a display of peppermint latte and chocolate mocha mint candles at the time. "No. No appliances. Sorry."

Third place, tires.

"Do you carry radial tires?"

I've never really understood radial tires. Tires, I get. I drive around on four all the time. But radial means circle, right? Circles are round. Aren't all tires round? Doesn't that make all tires radial tires?

"No," I say. "We don't carry radial tires." Or any other tires.

Fourth place: specialty kitchen items.

Customer: "Do you sell woks?"

Me: "Ewok? Like Star Wars?"

Customer: "W-O-K-S. Woks. You know. Stir fry? Woks?"

Me: "No. No woks."

Customer: "Well, you're missing a good opportunity. You should sell woks."

Me: (I got nothing.)

Customer: "How about programmable rice cookers? Do you sell programmable rice cookers?"

If we didn't sell woks, why would we sell programmable rice cookers?

To the public at large, what we buy is as confusing as what we sell. One of my favorite questions or I should say one of my most frequently asked questions is, "Do you buy antiques?"

"No. I'm not an antique dealer."

"But wait," they say. "It's a Duncan Phyfe sofa." Then without fail, they go on to describe the sofa in detail, and when they're done, I'm still not an antique dealer. I know antique dealers. I'm happy to refer Duncan Phyfe people to local antique dealers, but still—I hear it all the time—they'd rather sell it to me.

Why? I do not know.

Often, people who want to sell me oddities smaller than sofas show up with them. Once, and the absolute worst, was an elephant footstool. And I'm not talking about a footstool covered in fabric depicting cuddly baby elephants. It was the actual chopped-off *foot* of an actual *elephant* made into an actual *stool*. It was horrifying, and it was a hard no.

We get our fair share of treasure sellers too.

Antiques Roadshow Fan: "I have a Sorry! board game from 1950."

Me: "And?"

Antiques Roadshow Fan: "It has all the original pieces."

Me: "Wonderful."

Antiques Roadshow Fan: "Elvis played it."

Me: "Really?"

Antiques Roadshow Fan: "Yes. It was my aunt's and she met Elvis."

And they played Sorry!?

Antiques Roadshow Fan: "Do you want to buy it?"

Me: "I'm not an antique dealer."

Antiques Roadshow Fan: "Well, if you were an antique dealer, what would you pay me for it?"

Me: "I don't appraise antiques either. I have no idea what it's worth."

Antiques Roadshow Fan: "I also have a handwritten baguette recipe from the French Revolution. Would you be interested in that?"

I find it highly unlikely that a handwritten recipe from the late 1700s could escape France and find its way to Main Street in Chattanooga, Tennessee, two hundred years later. I passed.

Something else we don't buy? Furniture. We don't buy used furniture. Some days, half our phone calls are furniture calls.

"Do you buy furniture?"

"No."

"Yes, you do."

"No, I'm sorry. We don't."

"I read it online."

"Not on our Facebook page, our Instagram account, or our website."

"It's on your Google."

"Sir, we don't have 'a Google,' per se."

"Yes, you do. I'm looking at it."

It's not just furniture. Google once got me into a hash-brown argument that wouldn't stop.

"Do you have frozen hash browns?"

"We're not a grocery store."

"Google says you are."

Thanks again, Google.

Don't get me wrong. I google as much as the next guy. How to spell pharaoh. How to spell handkerchief. How long does it take to drive to Miami? Why does my right eyebrow grow faster than my left eyebrow? (Don't ever ask Google a question like that because the first answer is always brain tumor.) For the most part, I take Google results with a grain of salt and a dash of common sense. Hash Brown Woman didn't.

"It says right here on Google that you're a grocery store."

"Ma'am, I can assure you we're not."

It was like she wanted to talk me into being a grocery store. It was like she thought she could wear me down, and I'd eventually confess to being a grocery store. I promise you, if I'd had frozen hash browns in my freezer just then, I'd have let her win. I'd have given her my hash browns and let her believe they were from a grocery store. Because at that point, I really wanted to meet her.

"If you don't have frozen hash browns in your grocery store, do you know the closest one that would?"

Closest to what? Me? Her?

"I have to have them. I'm having a party."

"Try Publix," I said.

"Good idea," she said.

It was one of those times I called Tech Support, who I also like to call Sweet Angel Child from Heaven. "Somewhere on Google, we're listed as a grocery store. Can you fix it?"

Sweet Angel Child from Heaven said, "Scoot over." She clicked the keyboard for two seconds. "I googled 'grocery stores in my area,' and we're listed as number seven. Four hundred seventy-one people found us last month by googling 'grocery store.' Only one hundred seventy-three found us by googling 'shopping near me.'"

"How is that possible?" I looked a little closer. "Leave it."

Sweet Angel Child from Heaven gave me her deadpan look.

I said, "We have a four-point-six rating as a grocery store," I said. "Let's not ruin a good thing. Four-point-six isn't anything to sneeze at."

And according to Google, we don't just sell groceries. We're a consignment shop too.

Several years ago, a fabulous review of Merchants on Main hit the internet. Five stars with this comment: "I love this cute consignment store!"

What magic word in that review would you imagine Google picked up and ran with? Consignment. Like our grocery-store status, the consignment review stands. The consignment phone calls are offset by the five stars.

"Will you sell my sofa for me?"

No.

"Can you sell my grandmother's furniture?"

Um, no.

"Will you sell my clawfoot bathtub?"

No.

For every three consignment calls, there's always one who won't let it go. "You advertise that you sell on consignment."

I explain that we don't. A reviewer said that. Not us. There are good consignment dealers out there, and

God love 'em, because the hard truth is if you don't want it, if no one in your family wants it, if you can't find a friend who wants it, chances are *no one wants it.*

You know the expression the only bad questions are the ones you don't ask? It doesn't necessarily apply to retail. My point? I will never sell car parts. (Or appliances. Or tires. Or your grandmother's sofa. Or hash browns.) But I will always sell adorableness.

WHERE DO YOU GET YOUR STUFF?

UNDER THE CATEGORY OF FREQUENTLY ASKED Questions, this is the one I hear most often.

We have more than twenty dealers who rent space at Merchants on Main. Each dealer has a booth, and every booth is special. Some go to auction for their merchandise, some go to estate sales, others to the market in Atlanta. Each booth reflects the taste and personality of the dealer. No two booths are the same, so there's something for everyone. As for me and Sweet Angel Child from Heaven, it's almost the same playbook. Most of our items come from auctions, from We Know a Guy, or from the market in Atlanta.

There are several auctions we never miss. Some are in the middle of nowhere, others just down the street. Each is different. Did we really need to bid on ginormous granny panties with a rebel flag on the butt? Probably not. But the same auction the next week might have treasure after treasure on the auction block. I can spot a diamond in the rough, the perfect item to restore.

Afterward, of course, I turn it over to my artistic daughter. She works her magic on the neglected dresser, armoire, or coffee table, and out the Merchants on Main door it flies with a new lease on life. Madi has a gift with color and design. Her mother does not. I handle the front end, she handles the back end, and we call that perfect harmony.

One of my favorite auctions is just down the street. After a decade of working side by side with the owners, they've become family. My adopted big brothers. They've taught me so much, like what to say to mean boys, how to parallel park, and how to sneak in and out without Mom and Dad ever knowing. Kidding. But I have learned from them what to look for and what to avoid in a piece of furniture. They've taught me the art of bidding. They've taught me the fun of auctions. (Not just because they serve food and wine.) (But it helps.)

I love the surprise of their auctions. I've seen them auction off cars, every imaginable and unimaginable piece of furniture, jewelry to die for, and stunning works of art. Once, it was a boat. (I didn't bite. I already had a boat. *Voyage of the Damned*—but that's another story.) The most bizarre item I've ever seen them present was a movie prop. A flying monkey from *The Wizard of Oz*. Yes. *The Wizard of Oz*. Can you imagine turning on a light to see that staring at you in the middle of the night?

At auctions, I look for furniture to flip. Just the right piece at a great price. Bidding wars happen. Sometimes, it's all in fun, and other times, it's not pretty. One rule I have is that I never bid against a Merchants on Main customer. If they want the piece, it's theirs. There'll be another auction the next week.

We Know a Guy. We met him years ago. He goes by the name Small Change. The first time he pulled his truck into the parking lot, I was skeptical. He didn't look like my typical shopper. I soon learned that in addition to being the wheeler-dealer I thought he was at first glance, he was a treasure hunter too. He could find anything. A gold velvet three-seater sofa? No problem. A hot-pink chaise lounge? Coming right up. A sideboard with cone-shaped legs? He'd be back with one the next day. There were times he hit it out of the ballpark. Other times, not so much, but hey, a pair of groovy swivel chairs in giraffe print might not be on planet Earth to be found.

When I say he can find anything that is out there, I mean it. He can. Even life things. When Sweet Angel

Child from Heaven needed a new microwave, there he was with one. New washer and dryer? There they were on the back of his truck. Once, I thought about asking him for something way out there, like a vampire coffin, just to challenge him, but knowing he'd be back in a matter of hours with an actual vampire coffin, I didn't. What would I do with it?

We have our secret shopping spots too. The metal menagerie of animals we own and sell come from a place far, far away, in the middle of nowhere, at the end of a long gravel drive. There are acres and acres of anything and everything you could imagine. I rent a cargo van, and we drive down early in the morning and return late in the afternoon. Need a twelve-foot-tall dragon? Check. A two-story rooster? Check. A metal elephant the size of a, well, elephant? We have one right here. We've purchased a barnyard of flying pigs, goat mamas and babies, and of course, flamingos.

The trip is an adventure we look forward to—Sweet Angel Child from Heaven and her mother in the van together for hours and hours on end. Apparently, I talk too much in the mornings. Must be the coffee. The ride home is quieter with all the metal animals listening intently in the back of the van. The ride home is faster too. Because we're ready for cocktails.

Atlanta. AmericasMart Atlanta. The *world's* largest collection of wholesale gifts, décor, and apparel right down the road. (Two hours down the road.) It's hard to explain how big it is. Three monstrous buildings, each twenty stories tall, and every inch absolutely stuffed with goodies. My friend and Merchants on Main dealer, Mims, and I have gone together for years. One year, Sweet Angel Child from Heaven wanted to join us. I warned her beforehand.

"Madi, get ready to walk."

"I know how to walk. I've been at it a while."

"Miles, Madi. Miles and miles and miles and miles. And that's just one building. There are three. All those miles times three. Wear your good tennis shoes. We leave at dawn."

"Oh, no, we don't," said my daughter who doesn't do dawn. "I'll meet you there at a decent hour."

Well, I tried to warn her, but at some point, you have to let them go their own way. You know what I mean? By the time we met up, the only thing she said to me that I can repeat in print was, "I'm calling Human Services."

(She was legal in every state.)

(Past legal in every state, as a matter of fact.)

We had hotel rooms that weren't exactly next door to each other. The only way for Madi to meet me was to drive to the hotel and take the train downtown.

Alone. Another thing I warned her about. I gave her tips and tricks for navigating the train. I told her to look for people wearing AmericasMart badges and stick close to them.

I'm not sure what exactly happened on that train, but when she finally reached me, people started backing away and looking for security.

Madi's voice carried. And she had a lot to say. About the speed of the train— (she was sure she had whiplash), about her fellow train travelers (some most certainly dead), about the terrifying tunnels (Like Disney Hell), about the beggars (she did not give money to the guy in her face repeatedly demanding $3.27 for a McDonald's biscuit), about the drunks (the fumes were unbearable and she might never drink again), about the public nudity (she was scarred for life), about the sexual escapades (ruining her chances of a healthy relationship forever), about the gravity-defying elevator ride from train hell to fresh air only to land in the middle of a Save the Damn Whales protest.

She loves whales.

Then she asked why I hadn't warned her.

I had. I opened my mouth to remind her when out of nowhere, a New Orleans marching band started up and paraded around us in their costumes, feather boas, beads, tutus, and umbrellas.

Somehow, she managed to make herself heard over their saxophones and tubas. “It’s bad luck to open umbrellas inside!”

I did what any good mother would do. I led her straight to a refreshment stand because she needed refreshing. I let her drink frozen margaritas until her color returned.

Sweet Angel Child from Heaven is now a seasoned market pro. She invited her adopted big brother, the Pumpkin, and he helps pick out great Merchants on Main treats too. Come by and see what just came in today!

BONES IN THE BACKYARD

ANOTHER YEAR CAME AND WENT. THE GREEN LEAVES turned to brilliant reds, deep oranges, and vibrant golds. Sweaters woke from hibernation. Pumpkins popped out on porches. And that meant it was time to get the store ready for the holidays. It was time for a deep clean.

In retail, we don't spring clean. We fall clean. The truth is we clean around the clock but with a special emphasis on the holidays. That year, as usual, we cleaned inside and out to prepare for our holiday open house. That meant replanting the flowerpots outside because, after an unusually hot and busy summer, everything in them was a crispy shade of death.

I lined up Ace, a gentle giant of a man and a trusty

right arm with a strong back, to help me tackle the exterior. His day job was gardening-adjacent, so he knew what he was doing. I could tell he was trying not to judge me for murdering all the plants in the flowerpots because Ace takes gardening seriously *and* personally. To him, I'd killed his children. He didn't say anything, but he gave me lots of side-eye, and when he wasn't doing that, he was shaking his head. In spite of his quiet disappointment, we made excellent progress, and eventually, the exterior of Merchants on Main looked like something just shy of a Disney property. It was time to move on to the hard part. The fenced-off area behind the store.

I don't know how or why the backyard catches everything, and by the time we get around to cleaning it, it always looks like a cross between a garden that grows trash and an abandoned-item cemetery watched over by the creepiest of abandoned items, the boat.

Why do we have a boat in the backyard? At this point, I barely remember.

A friend (I'm being generous. Maybe I should say an acquaintance?) asked if we could store his boat for a few weeks. A few weeks? Sure. That was eons ago. To this day, there sits the sailboat in my backyard. He never returned for the boat. I haven't heard a word from him. Through the years, the elements have taken their toll on the boat. At this point, I can't look at it without thinking of the Bermuda Triangle. *The Poseidon Adventure.* The Titanic.

We call it *Voyage of the Damned.* It's been there so long it's probably home to damned woodland creatures or, more likely, damned rats. I wouldn't know because I've never worked up the nerve to examine it that closely. For all I know, it could be full of pirate treasure. Ahoy, matey.

Ace and I were making great progress around the haunted sailboat. We'd almost finished clearing the broken furniture, wet cardboard, wooden pallets, and a box of cushions that had somehow made their way out back. I wish I knew how things got there in the first place. The backyard is often the subject of Merchants on Main's not-me game.

Me: "Who threw a decoupage bookcase out back?"

Everyone Within Earshot: "Not me." "Not me." "Not me."

Me: "Who threw an avocado-green plastic sink out back?"

Everyone Within Earshot: "Not me." "Not me." "Not me."

Me: "Who threw a very questionable queen-sized mattress out the back door?"

Everyone Within Earshot: "Not me." "Not me." "Not me."

Apparently, these things dropped out of the sky. I've learned to move on. There are times I think about repurposing the backyard. Maybe plant a few Japanese maple trees, add a bench, and call it a park. It could be a habitat for cute little animals like chipmunks. Or hedgehogs. It would be a great space for a small carnival ride, like a merry-go-round. Or maybe a cute gazebo. Anything but the graveyard it is.

Ace and I worked hard. Our mission was almost complete. We were exhausted, filthy, and felt good about a job well done. It was as I reached for the very last piece of trash that I saw the bones.

Cue the soundtrack for every horror movie ever filmed.

Cue my heart almost beating out of my chest.

Cue full-volume sailor language.

I'd found a skeleton. A freaking skeleton. A *skeleton* in the backyard.

Ace came running.

It didn't look human, so we didn't call the police. There were no news crews. No Duckie from *NCIS*. No cold-case detectives. Just me and Ace.

It was a large skeleton with a spine and a tail. Maybe.

It had no head.

When we calmed down enough to make our next move, we knew exactly what it would be or rather *who* it would be. We needed Sweet Angel Child from Heaven. We found her at the front desk, ringing up sales and wrapping gifts. I knocked the worst of the dirt off my boots, took a deep breath—didn't want to alarm the customers—and walked calmly to the register. I fiddled. Pasted the fakest of smiles on my face. I waited patiently for the store to clear of customers.

She was onto me already. "What now?"

"Madi, honey?" I cleared my throat. "Could you take a look at something outside?"

Ace stood behind me for moral support.

She said, "Oh hell."

She knows me that well. She'd handled an army of frogs hopping through the store, more mice than could ever be counted, and a mangled bunny in the parking lot. She had a good idea as to what I needed her to take a look at. She steeled herself and said, "Lead the way."

The three of us trudged out back.

She tilted her head this way then that way, all without screaming, and announced, "I have no clue."

The thing is, she's an animal lover, particularly horses. She's an accomplished rider from way back. She's connected to animals in a way I'm not. I think it's why she's so handy solving animal problems. But staring at the headless carcass of an unknown animal, she hesitated. She looked at Ace, Ace looked at me, and I looked at Sweet Angel Child from Heaven.

"The bones have to go," I said.

"You're the *CSI* fan, Mom," Sweet Angel Child from Heaven said.

"This"—I pointed—"is not a television show. This is real-life dead. I'm not touching it."

We both looked at Ace, who said, "Don't look at me."

By unanimous decision, we decided to leave the bones where we found them. After all, whatever it was chose our backyard as its final resting place. We thought it best to honor its wishes.

A good friend, I call her Ms. Africa, once told me about a tradition in her country. Whenever anyone happened upon a dead snake, they chopped it up, set it on fire, then scattered the charred remains to frighten off other snakes. We had nothing to chop, and we weren't about to build a ceremonial fire or scatter anything, but we did like the idea of our bones warding off other wild beasts.

The bones might still be out there.

I haven't looked.

Even once.

After work, we held a memorial service of sorts at our neighborhood bar down the street. Rest in peace, whatever you were.

REAL
SOLID
DUDE
4
5
6
10
11
12
16
17
18

NMBF (NOT MY BOYFRIEND)

If you work at Merchants on Main, and you're under the age of thirty, you're one of my kids. That's how it is. Not only are my kids the most creative people alive when it comes to why they're late to work—a convoy of armadillos shut down Gunbarrel Road, and they had to find an alternate route; there was a sinkhole in the Starbucks drive-through, and they were two tires in and two tires out, waiting on their caramel macchiato; their cat might be pregnant, and they were at the vet's, waiting on the cat pregnancy test results—they find interesting ways to entertain themselves when they are at work.

A favorite subject of theirs is my love life. (Or lack thereof.) Over the years, interesting men have wandered through our door. And while I can't put my finger on exactly when it started, the kids got it in their heads that any unaccompanied man who stepped into the store was there for me and only me. "Mom? Is that your boyfriend?"

Not My Boyfriend #1. A man I'd never seen in my life walked in the front door and straight to the desk. "Are you dating anyone?"

Out of absolutely nowhere. And there's an audience. Customers shopping near the front desk. Their ears perk. What a treat. Shopping and a show.

I started and stopped several times then finally chose "Not really."

NMBF #1 immediately followed up with "Are you married?"

(Seriously?)

"Well, it's complicated," I told him, even though it's none of his business.

My ambiguous answers, two in a row, were meant to convey I'd rather keep my private life just that, private, because keep in mind my customer audience. (Who had pulled up chairs and were passing popcorn.) I was a shop owner. I couldn't be outright rude to the man. And he wouldn't let it go. He wanted the gory details. So did the popcorn women.

NMBF #1 says, impatiently and with huffy breath, "Either you are, or you're not."

Which was when I wanted to ask if his way of

introducing himself to women ever worked. Not that I'm an expert at asking people out. In my life, I've only asked a guy out once. It didn't go well. I learned my lesson. From that point on, I've let God, the universe, and serendipity take the wheel of my dating life, but that day, karma jumped in. And what I did to someone for karma to trap me and make me feel that uncomfortable in my workplace with customers and kids all around who clearly thought they were witnessing a meet-cute, I don't know. But NMBF#1, after having me off my game since he walked in the door, did it again. He asked for my number.

What choice did I have? A stack of business cards with my number on them was right in front of him. I passed him one.

He wasn't out of the parking lot before one of the kids said, "Mom? Is that your boyfriend?"

Not My Boyfriend #2. He's a regular. He frequents the store so often I don't remember when we met. I've gotten over the shock of his greeting, every single time: "I just got out of jail." It didn't matter who was standing there. It didn't matter that I was working. It didn't matter that I might be in the middle of a conversation. Every time, he led with: "I just got out of jail."

He stopped by often. Usually, to sell me something he'd found. (I've never once bought.)

"Maybe next time," I'd say because I knew there'd be a next time.

He was funny, entertaining, and always had a great story to go with the limited-edition Tonka truck or small oil painting of a man's big toe he wanted to pawn off on me.

One bright, shiny day, he burst through the door with his favorite line. "Well, I just got out of jail."

Me: "Oh? What did you do this time?"

NMBF#2: "It was my old lady. She called the law on me."

Me: "Your old lady? Do you mean your wife? I thought you two split up."

NMBF#2: "We did, and we didn't."

It was then I realized we were having this conversation around customers. I was so familiar with NMBF#2 that I forgot other people weren't. I glanced at two stunned ladies and gave NMBF#2 a push for the door. Outside, as he led the way to his truck, where I assumed I'd hear a story about a tackle box he wanted to sell me that might have been Ernest Hemmingway's, the jail conversation continued.

NMBF#2: "She came at me like a crazy person. I was just trying to defend myself, and the next thing I knew, I was in jail."

(He's more than six feet tall. Just throwing that into the mix.)

Me: "Sure."

Him: "You don't believe me?"

Me: "Maybe face facts that you two aren't good together."

Him: "Then what would I eat?"

We were almost at his truck.

Him: "There's someone I want you to meet."

Me, stopping dead in my tracks: "Is it your old lady?"

Him: "No. It's my boo."

I'm no marriage counselor, but it passed through my brain that his boo might be the reason his old lady went at him like a crazy person. Then it occurred to me his crazy old lady could be lurking nearby in an effort to send NMBF#2 back to jail. Or maybe *she* wanted to meet his boo. I thought it best to untangle myself from the domestic drama before I ended up in jail with all three of them.

When I had one foot back inside, it was the first thing I heard. "Mom? Is that your boyfriend?"

Not My Boyfriend #3. The fun doesn't just happen during business hours. One Sunday, the Pumpkin and I went to Costco. (The Pumpkin: best wingman ever, who I'd call for bail money, moonlights as a literary assistant.) We went to Costco because treasures could be found there too. Treasures and huge buckets of M&Ms Peanuts.

Like everyone else shopping that day, we bought nearly everything in sight. I was overdressed for the occasion in a vegan-friendly leopard, cheetah, or pink zebra jacket—I can't remember—tight straight skirt, and boots, but I liked buying two hundred rolls of paper towels for five dollars just as much as the guy wearing Liberty overalls.

Back at Merchants on Main, the Pumpkin helped me unload. I was one carton of olive oil in when my phone rang. It was a friend. Let's call her Chatty Cathy. Thirty seconds later, I was trying not to drop a ten-year supply of French's mustard while Chatty Cathy was almost through her first story about a total stranger in the hospital, all their gory symptoms, their prognosis (not good), and the poor state of hospital food.

There was no need for me to take part in the conversation. There never was. Chatty Cathy talked for me. And she never took a breath. I was inside, deciding what to do with a box of fifty thousand paperclips, while Chatty Cathy told me what was on her grocery list and why it was on her grocery list when I noticed a prostitute in the corner of our parking lot.

It's Main Street. And my parking lot is easy to find. It's a good hookup place.

The prostitute was on the phone. Just like me.

I was lugging enough Froot Loops to feed a church camp all summer while Chatty Cathy was in my ear, weighing the pros and cons of moisturizing shampoo versus conditioning shampoo when a pickup truck came racing into the parking lot. A man was behind the wheel and on his phone. Yelling. I didn't know if he was yelling at me or whoever was on the other end of his call. I only caught every fifth word because of Froot Loops, Chatty Cathy, and the prostitute in my parking lot. But when I pieced every fifth word together, it slowly dawned on me. He thought he was on the phone with me, in front of him, when he was actually on the phone with the prostitute behind him. I ran in and locked the door, leaving a case of Uncle Ben's Original Wild Rice in the parking lot to fend for itself. Chatty Cathy, who'd talked my ear off through it all, gave me good advice when I told her I had to get off the phone with her to call the potential-rape-situation hotline. If there was such a thing. She said, "Get out of there."

I did.

I ran across the street and grabbed my friend Ireland. I told her I needed a mimosa, and she did too. From our window seat at our favorite Sunday brunch spot, Ireland and I watched the prostitute circle the block, looking for her date, and the pickup truck circle the block, looking for *me*. He still thought I was his date. I took it as a compliment as I stared down the barrel of the Big Six-Oh and as a style compliment, too, because my boots were cute. I wasn't two sips into my mimosa when my phone rang. It was one of my kids. "Mom? Is that your boyfriend?"

There were others. Prison Pants. Yes, a man walked in Merchants on Main rocking prison pants. He looked like he'd just jumped off a train. Like in *Brother Where Art Thou?* The Southside backs up to the Chattanooga Choo Choo, so there are plenty of railroad tracks to go around. Prison Pants wandered around, leaving prison-escapee fingerprints all over the store, then left. Probably to catch his next train. I knew it was coming. "Mom? Is that your boyfriend?"

There was Skateboard Machete Man. Yes, a man passed through the parking lot on a skateboard, waving a machete. "Mom? Is that your boyfriend?"

But the worst was Serial Killer. You read that right. NMBF#5: Serial Killer.

We've all heard bad pickup lines, and I'm here to tell you I've been on the receiving end of the very worst. After a long day at work, starving, I walked down the street for dinner. I was alone at the bar of one of my favorite restaurants, catching up on neighborhood gossip with one of my favorite bartenders and enjoying one of my favorite wines, all just as God intended, when a man walked in and sat beside me. He looked like a very normal man. Maybe normal plus. He was wearing an oxford shirt and starched khakis, he was attractive, and he smelled like man soap. He got the conversation ball rolling perfectly by asking me about the Southside, one of my favorite subjects. He said he was in town on business. He was funny and friendly but not too funny or friendly. All was well, maybe better than well, until it wasn't. I can't put my finger on exactly when it took a wrong turn.

He was gazing into my eyes. Or I should say I thought he was gazing into my eyes. I thought wrong. He opened his mouth, and these words came out: "You have a beautiful vein that runs down your forehead."

I do? No, I don't. I've had the same head all my life, and it doesn't have a beautiful vein or anything else running down it.

Does it?

My hand flew to my head. I patted around for something unicorny. My brain tossed around the word *lobotomy*. Visions of the "Here's Johnny" scene of *The Shining*, with the ax, was playing in my mind, all interrupted by the freak beside me, who said, "Can I touch it?"

What, exactly, did he want to touch?

I was too blown away to answer. I shook my head. *Keep your hands to yourself, nutcase.*

That was when my adorable bartender noticed something amiss. She asked, "Are you okay?"

"Tab," I said. But I think it came out, "Kloop." I slid off the barstool and said, "Excuse me," to the psycho, but I think it came out, "Wroox." I made a run for the ladies'.

When the coast was clear, the bartender and I watched him cross the street for another bar, probably intent on totally unnerving another unsuspecting woman right before he slit her throat. It was my first and I hope last encounter with a serial killer. There wasn't a doubt in my mind he had something on his person soaked in chloroform.

After another glass of wine and serious dissection of the whole surreal encounter, my bartender and I started wondering how many bodies were chopped up in various freezers scattered around his basement. Should we case the neighborhood for a white panel van? Would we find ropes, shovels, and Clorox in it?

The next day, I called Sweet Angel Child from Heaven and the Pumpkin to the conference room. (Dead space beside the spiral staircase to nowhere.) We huddled. I gave them the terrifying highlights. Then I said, "Do I have a vein in my head?"

"Let's hope so," Sweet Angel Child from Heaven said.

The Pumpkin nodded along.

"A vein you can see?"

"Not right this minute," the Pumpkin said.

My hand flew to my forehead again. "What's that supposed to mean?"

"It pops out when you've had a few," Sweet Angel Child from Heaven, who always breaks it to me so gently, said.

"It does not." I turned to the Pumpkin.

He nodded.

"Why haven't either of you ever told me?"

Sweet Angel Child from Heaven shrugged. "How do you not know? It's your head. How do you not know your own head?"

The Pumpkin said, "I'm pleading the Fifth."

Sweet Angel Child from Heaven said, "Mom? Is he your boyfriend?"

FLAMINGOS

I HAVE A HEALTHY OBSESSION WITH FLAMINGOS. AT least I think it's healthy.

I sell flamingos at Merchants on Main and display ones from my personal collection on both sides of the front doors, in the front windows, and in the flower beds. I even have flamingos pulling Santa's sleigh at Christmas.

One morning, I found two new flamingos nestled beside the front door, which was a switch. Usually, things disappeared from outside the store. Seldom did they appear. But someone had left me two beautiful flamingos. Later, I learned they were a gift from a cute couple who lived in the neighborhood. From then on, I called the cute girl Flamingo Fairy.

The point I'm trying to make is that my flamingo game is strong.

One sunny Saturday morning, it was time to flip the sign to Open. We were ready for the day. The large metal flamingo, the baby goats, the roosters, and the rest of the metal menagerie at the front door were ready to greet customers. The Pumpkin arrived with delicious scones from our favorite family restaurant down the street. Ms. Africa dropped in for our regularly scheduled Saturday coffee talk. (Straight-up gossip.) All was right with the world when the phone rang.

The Pumpkin answered. "Thank you for calling Merchants on Main, where it's a super-sparkly day." A minute later, a confused look spread across his face. He said, "Thank you," hung up, then turned to me. One of our regular customers had called to say she was having brunch a few miles away and saw a strange couple pushing a shopping cart with what looked very much like my front-door flamingo riding shotgun. In the shopping cart.

I ran to check, and sure enough, not only was my flamingo missing, so were my baby goats. While we'd been enjoying scones, coffee, and gossip inside, my flamingo and two goats had been swiped outside.

Ms. Africa agreed to watch the store while the

Pumpkin and I raced to save the flamingo. (And the baby goats.)

Ms. Africa said, "Do you want me to call the police?"

My first thought was no because if it was a slow news day, I might end up a local headline—Southside Store Owner Has Massive Meltdown over Missing Flamingo—but I quickly changed my mind because it might not be as easy as tracking the couple down and saying, "Gimme my flamingo back, you freakin' flamingo thieves." What if they pulled it out of the grocery cart and started beating the Pumpkin over the head with it? The flamingo is as tall as I am. She's a big girl. There would be injuries.

I dialed 911.

I led with an apology, certain the police had better things to do than chase a flamingo down Market Street. But to my surprise, the female dispatcher said, "Not at all. The police are already looking for the couple. We've had several calls this morning. They're pillaging the Southside. In addition to stealing everything that isn't nailed down, they're digging up entire gardens. Where were they last seen?"

I told her.

She said there were police cars already in the vicinity, and she'd send them our way. She advised us not to approach the couple. Wait on the police.

The Pumpkin rummaged through the car for trench coats, night-vision goggles, and weapons, none of which we had, when I popped him on the arm. "There they are."

And there was my flamingo, her head dangling off the side of the shopping cart. The Pumpkin and I hit the floorboard so they wouldn't see us. We eventually worked up the nerve to peek over the dash, knowing the criminals would escape if we didn't somehow manage to get our brave on enough to look.

I dialed 911 again to tell the authorities we had eyes on the perps. I told the same lady who'd taken my first flamingo emergency call that the bad guys were probably on the verge of committing yet another felony because they were crawling through the shrubs in front of an office complex.

"Now he's climbing a tree," I said. "He's ripping off branches with his bare hands and dropping them in the shopping cart."

She said, "Could you speak up? I doubt they can hear you from a block away. You don't need to whisper."

Beside me, the Pumpkin was sweating bullets, and I'd never heard him breathe that fast.

Just then, the cavalry arrived.

We fell in behind the officers. (Way behind.) I might have been dragging the Pumpkin by his ear and against his will. We arrived at the crime scene mid-interrogation. The officer, seeing us, switched gears. "Did you steal this woman's flamingo?"

All eyes turned to me.

Female Shopping Cart Thief said, "Baby, was that your flamingo?"

"Yes."

"Girlfriend..." She leaned in to take me into her confidence. "I took it for Jesus." She went on to explain, dropping Bible names the whole time—Shadrach, Meshach, and Abednego—why she stole for Jesus. Apparently, Jesus told her to steal my flamingo.

Under his breath, the Pumpkin said to me, "She's trying to establish an insanity defense."

"Step aside," the officer said to Jesus's Thief. "Let this woman get her belongings out of your cart. Jesus will understand."

One of the officers helped me dig through the cart. Nothing made any sense. I found my baby goats under a ceramic hedgehog and on top of carrots ripped straight from the ground by their long, leafy stems. Under a mailbox full of someone's mail, I found half my flamingo. I hauled her out of the buggy then hid behind a big strong officer. I stuck my head out to ask the flamingo kidnapper who claimed to be working for Jesus, "Where are her legs?"

She pointed.

My flamingo's legs were propped against a tree. Abandoned. Sacrificed to make room for the branches they'd been stealing when we caught them. Beside me, I guess at the sight of my flamingo's detached limbs, the Pumpkin took a seat and dropped his head between his knees. He'd had enough. I gathered my flamingo, her legs, my baby goats, and my Pumpkin and left the crime scene.

Back at the store, I asked Ms. Africa what I'd missed.

"A lady looking for flamingo lamps."

Of course.

That night, over large glasses of wine, I told my friend Ireland about Flamingo Day, and just when I thought I'd reached the end, in walked the cute couple who'd gifted the baby flamingos to me way back when. You know. Flamingo Fairy? As it turned out, she was the saint who'd called the store that morning to report my flamingo riding down Market Street in a shopping cart. It was a full-circle moment. We raised glasses to toast a new Southside super-sparkly line if there ever was one, Stealing for Jesus.

RESTROOM
SCENE-DO NOT ENTER CRIME SCENE-DO NOT ENTER CRIME SCENE-DO NOT ENTER

THE BATHROOM

WARNING: THE FOLLOWING CHAPTER CONTAINS SCENES some readers might find disturbing. I know I certainly do. And with that being said, let's talk about the bathroom.

Over the years, I've dealt with bathroom issues that should have prepared me for anything. Among them, abandoned granny panties, the man we call Father Bathroom Time, and the kid who tried to flush a whole roll of toilet paper during our holiday open house. None of it prepared me for Giant Poo Man.

I was away for the day, and that almost never happened. My friend Mims and I were in Atlanta, shopping for new items for the store at Americas-Mart. We're a perfect shopping team. We spotted the same items at the same time, like snarky socks, anything funny related to adult beverages, and the occasional totally inappropriate items. After a successful day of shopping, we were ready for dinner. We had our Atlanta favorites, and that day, we'd chosen Italian. One glass of Chianti Classico in, Sweet Angel Child from Heaven called to (ruin my dinner) tell me what I'd missed. Giant Poo Man was what I'd missed. And I'd just ordered an antipasto salad and Caprese chicken entree.

"What happened?" I reached for my Chianti.

"First of all, he was so big I didn't think he'd fit through the bathroom door, but somehow, he managed. Second, he stayed there for almost three days. Third, when he finally came out, he said we needed a plunger."

No one in retail wants to be asked for a plunger. Ever.

No one *alive* wants to be asked for a plunger. Ever.

As it turned out, we didn't need a plunger. We needed a whole new building. In a different state. Maybe one of the M states. Michigan or Missouri or Montana. It wasn't the first time the toilet had clogged, and it wouldn't be the last, but it was without a doubt the most epic.

I reached for my Chianti again. "Did you give him the plunger?"

"Mom, he didn't ask for the plunger. He said we

needed a plunger. Big difference. He said we needed a plunger and left."

"Oh hell."

She went on to tell me she found the plunger, cracked the bathroom door, slammed it shut, slapped an Out of Order sign on the door, cordoned off the area with crime scene tape, and ran for the hills.

Next, she called Clogs R Us and told them it was a dire emergency. Three of their finest arrived. Three men with cast-iron stomachs, three men made of absolute steel, three men who deserved more money than they made, regardless of how much they made. Three men who went on to successfully have their way with our toilet. Not our bathroom. Just our toilet. And that was because of the Clogs R Us fine print, which sort of said, "Occasionally, the process of unclogging an unbelievable whopper of a clogged toilet will include a small or possibly large-ish reverse blast from the toilet. In other words, to get everything going the right way, the poo in question might go the wrong way, in every direction you can possibly imagine, and Clogs R Us doesn't do reverse explosive poo cleanup. We don't mind blockbuster poos, because we like challenges and need stories to tell our fantasy football buddies, but we don't stay for the aftermath. That's on you."

You, in the case of Giant Poo Man versus Merchants on Main, was me.

On the way home from Atlanta, having barely touched my dinner after all the poo talk, I gave myself a pep talk. It couldn't be that bad. I'd survived questionable high school and Las Vegas restrooms. I'd housebroken puppies. I'd changed diapers. None of which prepared me for our bathroom that night.

You're familiar with a semiautomatic rapid-fire confetti gun? Big barrel? Confetti goes everywhere? Up? Down? All around? It was like that, but it wasn't confetti. It was hell on earth. I will spare you the gory details except to say that by then, everything had congealed, I learned my gag reflexes were working properly, and I didn't sell a candle that would, well, hold a candle to the aroma.

I felt certain Giant Poo Man had left our store and checked himself into a nearby ICU, and on his admission paperwork, he wrote, "Something is bad wrong with me." Because something was bad wrong with that man. A solid two hours later, after burning my clothes and everything in the bathroom, including the sink, I took a Silkwood shower then texted the traumatized kids who'd worked that day.

Me: "Dear Sweet Mother of God. I just finished cleaning the bathroom. It was like a scene from *The Exorcist*. I have PTSD."

The kids: "Get a bottle of wine."

Me: "I've had two."

The kids: "We warned you. And we wrote it down in The Book."

(The Merchants on Main incident book. We keep it under lock and key. Trust me, you don't want to be an entry in The Book.)

Me: "I'm open to ideas about how we move forward after this."

The kids: "Maybe we should close the store."

Me: "We might have to. There isn't enough Clorox. There isn't enough sage to burn. Maybe we could set up in the parking lot. Does anyone have Porta Potty connections?"

The kids: "We will pray for your soul."

Me: "Just tell me this. Did he buy anything?"

The kids: "No."

The aftermath: Giant Poo Man was banned from our store for life. I cleaned the bathroom two more times that night and was forced to retire my favorite pink gloves.

I still miss my favorite pink gloves.

THE DAY OF THE OPOSSUM

THE DAY OF THE OPOSSUM SHALL GO DOWN IN INFAMY. That sounds better if you imagine Morgan Freeman saying it. And the day of the opossum started the night before. Once upon a time, we had the sweetest lab named Ruby. Her whole body wiggled, and her tail swung like crazy when anyone spoke to her. That's how full of love she was.

Ruby had many talents. She was an amazing swimmer. She could glide through the water like an otter. We loved to watch her swim. We would take her on field trips to a neighborhood pond. It was her favorite. Ours too. Until the day she took a pristine white duck into her mouth and dove under the water with it. (Cue screams from the shore.) We left as soon as she came up for air. The duck never resurfaced.

Ruby also had a great nose. She would plow through a field of flowers in full bloom, her tail going wild, her joy apparent. It was a sight to see her leaping in delight with a smile on her face as she hopped through sweet-smelling blossoms. On the other hand, Ruby was equally attracted to the vilest of smells, especially anything dead. The deader the better, said Ruby. She wiggled and said in Labrador language, "Look! Look! Look what I found!" She quivered at the discovery of decay. She would have made a fabulous cadaver dog. She would probably have run for corpses like I run for taco trucks.

On Opossum Eve, after our last walk, Ruby was more than her usual level of excited for her bedtime treat. She actually had a glow about her. A gleam in her eye. I knew she'd smelled something fascinating near the back doorsteps. She'd been fixated on that exact location. I had a hard time dragging her away, and once inside, she paced restlessly and, like I said, glowed. She was still thinking about whatever was underneath the steps. I don't doubt what she dreamed about that night.

The next morning after kibble, Ruby nearly knocked me down to get to the back door. It was then I got a whiff of whatever she'd smelled the night before, and it wasn't pretty. There was death at the back door. Ruby shot off like a rocket and disappeared under the stairs. She found the object of her affection. Something rotten and ripe. Somehow, I was able to drag her away from the steps and put her inside her fence.

Let me interrupt myself to explain Merchants on Main's Division of Duties. If it happened inside the building, generally, it was mine. I took care of cleanups on aisle five. They weren't all easy or pleasant jobs, but they were mine. When it came to nearly dead or all the way dead (inside or out) (human or animal), Sweet Angel Child from Heaven was in charge.

I couldn't. I just couldn't. There was something about making physical contact with the dead that sent me running for the hills. Screaming the whole way. My daughter, braver than me by far, didn't love the job, but she didn't lose her mind either.

I broke the news gently. "We need Animal Control out back."

"We?"

"Well, me," I said. "I need you."

She said, "Mom, you're a chicken."

"No, honey. It's bigger than a chicken."

She stomped off, still calling it a chicken. Or maybe she was still calling *me* a chicken.

She was gone longer than usual. She returned with a look of horror on her face. She said something along the lines of, "No way. Not happening." She went on to tell me she couldn't get to it if she wanted to, and even if she could, removing a dead something that big was above her pay grade.

A lively debate ensued between me and myself while Sweet Angel Child from Heaven silently stood her ground. How long might it take the dead thing to… go away on its own? Could we tough it out? What was our scented candle inventory right then? Did we know anyone who owed us a big, big, *big* favor? Did Chattanooga have an active Unalive Animal Rights Activist chapter that might help? Surely they would want whatever it was to have a proper burial. What about the fire department?

In the end, I asked my daughter, considering she'd already told me she couldn't get it out, if she could possibly scoot it somewhere else. Somewhere far, far away.

Nope. She declared getting it and scooting it to be the same thing.

By then, it was time to open the store and greet customers, and by unanimous decision, we decided to pretend there wasn't a large dead animal under the back steps.

Well, it was summer. The mercury climbed. We were at the point of lighting a match and burning down the whole place, which would surely take care of our problem, when a miracle walked in. It was one of our dealers stopping by with inventory. He was perfect for the job! He was just the ticket! There was no telling what he had buried in his backyard. (We suspected. But we'd never asked.) One thing was for sure. He was the type who wouldn't blink at a big dead thing under the back steps.

Let's call him Roadkill.

Roadkill was handy. And very outdoorsy. I wouldn't be surprised if he knew how to herd cows, rope bulls, and tame lions. Without a doubt, he knew how to load furniture. (Dead animals, furniture, six of one, half a dozen of the other, right?) He could stuff a normal truck with a small subdivision of furniture. He taught us how to load furniture without breaking a sweat. Or without breaking a glisten, as we Southern girls do. I know how to load furniture in heels, walking backward, all thanks to Roadkill. But loading furniture was just one of his talents. If he were a mobster, he'd be the one they called The Fixer. He was the kind of man who got things done. He didn't mince words either. I'd never ask him a question I didn't want the answer to. So when we explained our problem and asked if he could help, I knew our cadaver-under-the-stairs problem had been solved when he said a little more enthusiastically than the circumstances warranted, "Let's see this critter."

He nosed around our back room and found a shovel, a really long-handled shovel, like five feet long. I'd never seen it in my life, but I was glad to see it that day. Roadkill, armed with the long-handled shovel and a Hefty bag, took off to save the day. It wasn't over just yet, but we breathed a sigh of relief, and our day went back to somewhat normal. Sweet Angel Child from Heaven painted furniture, one of my beloved adopted kids rang up sales, and I wrapped gifts. But only until Roadkill returned, Hefty bag in hand, to stop a foot from me at the front desk and hold up the bulbous bag. "Opossum. What do you want me to do with him?"

(Did they make opossums *that* big?) (The Hefty bag was *stuffed*.)

It took me a moment to regain the gift of speech. "Outside." I pointed. "Outside, please," I choked out. "Garbage can." I pointed more. "Outside."

Ruby was heartbroken. Me? Not so much.

MY LIFE IS A ZOO

WHAT IS IT WITH ME AND ANIMALS?

We have the occasional slow day. Case in point, Wednesday. Wednesdays are generally slow days in retail. Although any day, slow or warp speed, has the chance to turn into a super-sparkly day, and it has an equally good chance of turning into an episode of *Wild Kingdom*. One minute, I'm minding my business in the truest sense of the phrase—I was minding my business—and the next, I didn't know if I should call Animal Control or the Chattanooga Zoo or go for my tranquilizer-dart gun.

One day, a friend stopped by to talk real estate on the Southside: who was buying, who was selling, who might buy, who might sell. Which always led down interesting roads like, "I heard he has a girlfriend," followed by "I heard *she* has a girlfriend," which landed on "They'll probably sell." "We should look at it first." "We should tell so-and-so."

You know. Chitchat.

In walked a gentleman I recognized. A man who stopped by every blue moon. He had an intense stare, and I'm not going to lie—it was creepy. He looked at me and stared then held the stare like a dare until I looked away. I glanced back, and he was still staring. Was he reading my mind? Zapping my brain cells? Surely not. Was he waiting for me to initiate conversation? Because I'm a pro at nervous mindless chatter. It's one of my gifts. In his case, I always had the feeling he was sizing me up. Like what would it take to stuff me into the trunk of his car. Great news that day—I wasn't alone in the store. I had Real Estate Guy, a few kids working, and customers.

Mr. Uncomfortable Stare was carrying a small plastic cooler. The cooler was full of baby ducks. You read that right. Baby ducks. He landed the cooler on the front desk next to the cash register, and small baby ducks poked their heads up, jack-in-the-box style. One little fuzzy head, then another, then another. He said, "When I saw these ducks, I immediately thought of you."

In what capacity? What did he see as my connection to baby ducks? Had we ever had a conversation about baby ducks? No. Had he overheard me saying I was in desperate need of a brood of baby ducks? No. Had he seen me wearing my three-carat yellow-diamond duck earrings? No. Because no one in their right mind owns three-carat yellow-diamond duck earrings. Including me.

Real Estate Guy struck up a conversation with Mr. Uncomfortable Stare. I'm not kidding. They started exchanging duck stories. Mr. Uncomfortable Stare, who I was in the process of renaming Duck Guy Who Stares, explained to Real Estate Guy that he had a pond on his property. (Why weren't the ducks in the pond? Why were they on my front counter, beside my cash register, where I needed to ring up sales to keep a roof over my head?)

I had to find a way to interrupt the duck chatter, lest it go on all day long, so I said, "Do you think the ducks need water?" As in *like a duck to water*. Everyone liked the idea. And it was the cutest thing, the baby ducks opening their baby beaks for their next drop. We were all admiring the ducklings drinking water when two real, live customers approached the front desk.

Real Estate Guy and Duck Guy Who Stares saw the ladies, too, but didn't budge an inch. They were busy with their duck stories. At the front counter of my store. With customers—customers holding merchandise and who had credit cards in their purses—waiting.

I finally had to wave. "Yoo-hoo. Do you mind?"

Duck Guy Who Stares said, "Not at all," but didn't move.

I finally had to ask them to move the duck party away from the front desk so I could work.

And with that, the duck spell that had been cast over Merchants on Main broke, and miracle upon miracles, the men and the ducks left. Except I had to explain it to the customers. "No, I don't sell live animals." And "I'm not sure if it's against health codes or not." And "I know one of them is in real estate. I'm not sure about the other, but I've never heard of a duck breeder. I think ducks breed themselves." It went on and on. And the thing was it was nowhere near Easter and nowhere near five o'clock.

When five o'clock finally arrived, I shared Duck Day with my friends over a tumbler of Grey Goose on ice.

The inexplicable happened all the time, and at the end of the day, I could usually find a drink to wash it all down. Now, Frog Day? I don't remember what I drank. Whatever it was, I drank a lot of it.

I already knew when I unlocked the doors and flipped the open sign, anything could happen. Anyone or anything could walk through the door. Frog Day started way earlier, before I ever had the chance to open the door. One morning, some might say middle of the night, our sweet black lab, Ruby, also known as my alarm clock, woke me with her tail thumping the side of the bed. She needed to step outside, she was starving, or maybe, looking back, she knew something was up downstairs.

I stumbled downstairs with her, half-asleep, half-dressed, and the minute my bare feet hit the store floor, I knew something wasn't right.

The floor jumped.

I woke up fast.

It was a frog. And he'd brought his friends. It was a plague of frogs of biblical proportions. Frogs *everywhere*.

While I was trying to figure out how all the frogs had found their way inside, Ruby was trying to figure out if it was her birthday. And the frogs were her present. Before I could grab her collar, she tried one. (*It was still dark outside. And inside. I was in my pajamas. And my dog ate a live frog.*) She liked it.

Ruby started gobbling frogs like it was her job. Who knew dogs liked frogs? I had to stop her because I didn't want to deal with her digestive issues, should the frogs not sit well on her tummy. (And in what world would live frogs sit well on a tummy?) I chased her, I yelled at her, I grabbed for everything I could get a grip on—her ears, her tail, her paws—and still, Ruby was faster than me and closer to the frog snacks.

Fast forward three hours you don't want to read about. Use your imagination.

That day, frogs kept popping up. I found one in the pottery booth. Another hopped along the ramp. Another was behind the front desk. Sweet Angel Child from Heaven stayed on frog patrol until they were all finally where they belonged, outside, and to this day, we have no reasonable explanation for Frog Day. That night, my bartender told me about a vodka-cranberry slushie drink called Frog in a Blender. I passed. I'm happy to say it never happened again, but I'm sorry to say scenes from Alfred Hitchcock's *The Birds* have.

You know those days that are so pretty you open all the windows? Can you see where I'm going with this? Birds? Windows? We don't necessarily have windows to open, but we do have doors. And on gorgeous sunny days, we throw them open. When the wind was blowing the wrong way, and the store filled with a nasty breeze straight from the chicken processing plant a mile away, we promptly closed them, but more often than not, it was fresh, clean, sunshine-kissed air. And birds.

Birds love to fly into the store. I don't know why.

We don't sell birdbaths or bird feeders, but they fly in anyway. If we're lucky, they fly right back out. If we're not lucky, they flutter around, trying to figure out where they are, how they got there, and how to get out. Their arrival gives me an eye twitch. When they flutter over, under, and through the pottery without breaking anything, we breathe sighs of relief.

Sometimes they find a perch and look so settled I'm tempted to put a price tag on them. They fly behind furniture, they land on chandeliers, and once, one stayed in the bathroom, banging his beak into the mirror, admiring himself for an hour. When they divebombed around the building into walls and displays, we freaked out, the customers freaked out, and it was all around freaky. Screaming at them didn't help because we don't speak bird. Shooing them toward the open doors only worked one time in ten. And nine out of ten of those times, the bird flew right back in through the other door, and the whole process started again. In the middle of a particularly long bird episode when we're exhausted, the bird is exhausted, and everyone's nerves are frazzled, we take a break and hide from the bird to (rest) formulate a better plan.

One of those times, a miracle occurred. Ms. Africa walked through the door.

"Where is everyone?"

We poked our heads up from behind the front desk. "We're hiding from a bird."

The bird was on the shelf of a bookcase, sitting so still he looked like a bookend. Ms. Africa calmly approached him, scooped him up in both hands, walked out the door with him, and set him free. It took her all of one minute to our hour. We now have her on speed dial under Bird Whisperer. That night, we drank Hummingbirds. A Hummingbird is champagne, a few ounces of St. Germain, which is a delicious liqueur made from elderflowers, and club soda. Highly recommended. Although not asking a cat if it's recently had kittens before you scare it off isn't recommended at all.

It was a Monday. Mondays, I work half days at the store and run errands the other half. That morning, I worked through my to-do list: yoga, check, haircut and color at the beauty parlor, check, bank, check. All within walking distance of the store. Getting my steps in. My reward for all those jobs well done was always a Diet Coke with extra ice from Sonic.

I grabbed the keys to Big Girl Truck. She's a beast, circa 1990-something, showing her age, and loved beyond measure. She's hauled enough furniture to fill a warehouse. She's hauled horse trailers and even a sailboat. (*Voyage of the Damned.*) She could haul several coffins at once, her bed deep enough to stack them if need be, not that I've ever thought about that. She had no air conditioning, which could sometimes be brutal in the middle of July, but she had amazing little windows—cigarette windows, my grandmother used to call them—that when positioned the right way made up for the lack of cold air. It was summer, and I'd left the cigarette windows open the last time I'd driven Big Girl.

I climbed into the cab. And when I say climbed, I mean it. Most of the time, I make the Pumpkin hoist me in. When he's busy, I get a step ladder. I have been known to get a running start and leap in. Big Girl is tall. I'm short.

I fired her up, cranked her into reverse, and was just about to take my foot off the brake when a cat flew at me from across the cab. She leaped onto the dashboard. It happened in a flash. I froze. Big Girl's huge steering wheel between us, the cat and I stared at each other. My voice was fourteen octaves higher than normal when I squeaked, "Kitty kitty?"

She flew out the cigarette window.

I had a mini stroke.

The whole way to Sonic, I thanked my lucky stars that I hadn't had a heart attack and died in Big Girl. No one would have found me for a week. Fifteen minutes later, on wobbly knees, with Sonic ice shaking in my cup loudly enough to wake the dead, I opened the store. The rest of the day went smoothly. Happy Hour rolled around, and it was time to put Big Girl to bed under her Big Girl carport. As I approached her, I heard something. Kitten somethings. I put it all together and realized the cat from earlier had kittens in Big Girl. Lovely. Now what? I put everything back where it was so the mother could find her kittens. I rolled all the windows down to give Mother Cat access then parked Big Girl exactly where she'd been that morning. Beside the sailboat. (*Voyage of the Damned* again.) My hopes and prayers were that the mother was waiting patiently to hop back in Big Girl, and they would all live happily ever after.

I called the Pumpkin to run it all by him.

"How many kittens?"

"I didn't look."

"Go look."

"I am not going back to Big Girl and running the mother off again."

"*You* are their mother now because you ran off their real mother."

"How is this my fault? Let me remind you I was only going to get a Diet Coke from Sonic."

"You scared the mother cat to death. She's not coming back. Go get your kittens out of the truck. They'll starve to death if you don't, Cruella, and you'll have killed a litter of kittens. Do you want that on your conscience?"

I did not.

I hung up on the Pumpkin and called Sweet Angel Child from Heaven. She had a much better attitude. For one, she didn't accuse me of being a kitten murderer, and two, she believed the mother cat would return. Then—by now you realize why I call her Angel Child from Heaven—she said she'd go to the pet store for cat and kitten things, whatever those were, and be there as soon as possible to make sure all was well with the mother and her kittens.

Take that, Pumpkin.

She found the kittens hidden in Big Girl. Four newborn kittens. Their eyes weren't even open. And the mother cat did return. Once during the night and then again the next afternoon. She relocated her kittens one by one to who knows where until there was only one kitten left. By then, we were living in the parking lot, binoculars glued to our eyes, tapping our feet, checking the time, and waiting patiently for the mother cat to return for her last kitten.

She didn't.

Night was falling. It would be cold. The newborn kitten wouldn't survive on its own.

The Pumpkin said to me, "I hope you're happy."

I smacked him. "This is not my fault."

Sweet Angel Child from Heaven to the rescue again. She took the kitten, bottle fed him, nurtured him, and named him. He joined her family. He wasn't her first foster fail. The kitten's big brother is a foster-fail dog. The kitten continues to grow. He's fearless. After his humble beginnings in Big Girl, he won the lottery. And he's spoiled rotten to prove it. Every once in a while, we toast Kitty with a Black Cat cocktail, which is a spiked cherry Coke. Delicious. And every once in a while, we observe a moment of silence for our beloved Dovey.

Once upon a time, we had a beautiful dove who lived at the store. She built her nest in one of the window ledges. We named her Dovey. As in Lovey Dovey. We had a perfect view of her from the front desk. It was like watching a YouTube channel of a bald eagle's nest, but Dovey was so much prettier. She returned every year to build her nest and have her babies. Our friends and customers knew Dovey and checked in on her regularly, especially when it was time for her eggs to hatch. We stayed on baby-dove watch every spring for years.

One year, as she was nesting, the weather forecast wasn't good. Worried about her, I dragged a tall sign from the front of the store to her nest on the side of the store to shield her from the approaching storms. She watched me with her trusting eyes, listened to me explain that I was protecting her and her babies, and what a sweetie, I think she knew I was trying to help. She didn't even leave her nest. She just watched me. When I had the sign in place, I swear she blinked thank you.

Once, a customer, stumbling on a Dovey conversation and realizing Dovey birthed her babies at Merchants on Main every year, asked me what Dovey did during her off-season. I said, "I guess she goes on vacation to Florida." (Isn't that what everyone does during their off-season?)

Dovey's last spring with us, she'd had another banner year. She had a nest full of fuzzy babies. Every morning, I checked on her, and every evening, I said good night to her sweet face. One night, after I'd locked up and was on my way to dinner, I noticed a hawk circling the parking lot. I didn't think much of it at the time, and even if I had, there wasn't much I could do, because I didn't have a shotgun on me, or at all, really, and if I had, chasing a hawk around a parking lot, blasting buckshot in the air, was frowned upon within city limits, but I'd have done it anyway, had I known, because the next morning, Dovey's nest was empty.

My heart stopped.

I ran outside. Feathers were everywhere. The nest was empty. No Dovey. No babies. That freaking hawk killed our dove family. But that wasn't the end of it. He continued to haunt me, as if he hadn't done enough already, lying in wait until he saw me then circling the parking lot over my head to remind me of what he'd done, and every time, I had a few choice words for him.

I may have flipped him off a few hundred times. I may have threatened him. I may have even gone a little crazy because of my broken heart and having to repeat the story over and over again to Dovey's fans. As time went on, and the hawk still wouldn't leave me alone, my hawk hate grew, and somehow, he knew it. The more I despised him, the more he taunted me.

It began to feel like a metaphor. A life metaphor. The innocent and trusting mother, living her best life, following the rules, taken down by the heartless and selfish predator who not only didn't care that he'd destroyed a family but also wouldn't go away after the destruction was done. And I didn't want to revisit the damage he'd done every single day. All I wanted was for him to go away and let me live my life without the constant reminder of his callousness and cruelty. But instead of going away, I kid you not, the hawk doubled down.

One day, soaring over me, reminding me again of what all he'd taken, the hawk gave back. His parting gift was a mangled bunny. He opened his nasty claws and dropped another life he'd destroyed to land almost at my feet. And like everything else I've been forced to face since the day she was born, Sweet Angel Child from Heaven was by my side to help clean up the mess he'd made. (She remembers my role in the cleanup a little differently. If you run into her, maybe don't bring it up.)

The moral of this story? Don't let the bastard hawks get you down.

The night of the mangled bunny, we drank everything in sight. The next morning, I dusted myself off and moved on with my life. I never saw the hawk again. If I do, I'll wring his neck.

LOST AND FOUND

I FIND THINGS. SMALL, LARGE, WANTED, UNWANTED, valuable, worthless, terrifying, some dead, many alive, I find them all. I find so many oddities in the parking lot, the flower beds, and strolling through the Southside neighborhood that one of my adorable waiters suggested I publish a coffee table book. I'm not sure how many people would want oversized glossy evidence of my finds on their coffee tables, but if I ever stumble across ten million dollars in unmarked bills or a stash of uncut diamonds or a map that leads me to a blowhole off Florida's Treasure Coast that's full of gold plus Matthew McConaughey minus Kate Hudson, I'll reconsider the coffee table book.

I find food. I often find jars of peanut butter on one of the large rocks in the parking lot. Rarely is there a lid. I always think about throwing the jar out, but a few days later, every time, someone takes the jar back.

The same thing happened with an open can of chili. The chili sat there for three days. It rained two of them. I was glad to see it had been claimed on day four because that watery chili was disgusting. Was someone feeding peanut-butter-and-chili-loving wildlife? In my parking lot? Was it some form of relationship, druggie, or international spy communication? ("If you see an open peanut butter jar in the Merchants on Main parking lot, the coast is clear. If you see an open can of chili, wait until you hear back from me.") Who chose that rock in my parking lot for a random food-signal spot?

The parking lot can turn into a closet, at times. Once, I found a pair of tennis shoes. Nice tennis shoes. I've found jackets, hats, socks, pajamas, gloves, bras, and once, men's undies. They weren't clean. We used tongs to transfer the undies to a shovel then built a parking-lot fire and burned it all—the undies, the tongs, and the shovel. After that, we showered in straight-up sanitizer.

One day, after a torrential downpour, the parking lot flooded. The water was at our doors. Cars continued to drive through the parking lot, causing a wake that splashed the water in. It was the closest our favorite backyard vessel, *Voyage of the Damned,* came to seagoing. When the water finally receded, we were left with a lot of mud and a rat skull. Not a mouse skull. A prehistoric rat skull. One of my adopted kids collects skulls (a chapter for a different book), and I gifted the skull to him. One of several skulls I've gifted him. So far, all animal.

Condoms. Nine out of ten times, they could have been sold as never worn. Very often, the package is open with the unused condom peeking out. I always wonder what happened. Did they change their minds? Get hungry? Did someone's wife, mother, or boss call? Did they lose interest? Once, I found three new condoms in a row. Connected. Like off a roll. Very rare. I usually find singles.

Hair weaves and extensions, very exciting. Exciting because every single time, I think it's a snake, until I realize someone's hair has fallen out of their head. On a city street. Not once has it been a real snake, but it could happen. One evening, I was out for a neighborhood stroll and almost stepped on a snake. I ran. I called Ms. Africa because the snake was near her mailbox. She went after it with a machete. (Yes, she owns a machete.) Five minutes later, she called to tell me it, too, was a hair weave. Dropped at her mailbox. She may have been sparing me the ugly truth, because I have evidence on my phone, and it still looks like a snake.

Death used to drop out of the sky regularly courtesy of the Hawk I Hated. Before the mangled bunny, it was shredded birds. Other times, piles of fur formerly worn by squirrels. Random chicken bones.

At least I hope they were chicken bones.

Once, I found a grown man sleeping on a rock. I didn't know what to do because there were no signs of life. Should I call the police? Nudge him with a broom? Go on my morning walk and do both if he was still there when I returned? While I tried to figure it out, he moved. I wondered if it was just post-death reflexes, but then he moved again. He was alive.

I let him sleep it off.

The scariest thing I've ever found was a shank. As in *prison shank*. Not that I'm an expert, but it looked a lot like the shanks you see in *Orange Is the New Black* or *Oz*. The handle was wrapped in dirty tape. The worst was where I found it. I was watering my flowers in front of the store only to discover my pretty pink flowers had been *stabbed*. That time, I did call the police. The shank was probably a key piece of evidence linking a killer to a murder. Right there in my flower bed. The police didn't come, unlike *CSI*, who'd have been all over it.

In the middle of all the condoms, discarded clothing, and open jars of peanut butter, some days, I'm rewarded with a flower. My favorite thing to find. A flower growing where it doesn't seem possible. With very little dirt but a lot of determination, a flower grows. It always reminds me of one of my favorite quotes: Bloom where you are planted. Yes! Just bloom!

I find things inside too. The usual things. Lip gloss and single-hoop earrings in the restroom. Empty coffee cups. Full coffee cups. Once, I found a half-eaten beef-and-bean burrito from Taco Bell on a soap display. Debit cards that slipped to the floor on their way into wallets at the front desk. At least three times a year, someone walks off and forgets their purchases. We've had pup shoppers leave, ahem, gifts, too, but better we find them than our customers.

For years, we had a dealer who would bring wooden, almost life-size children to display at Christmas. A boy and a girl. I'm not going to lie—they freaked me out a little from the beginning. Their eyes followed me. Like *Mona Lisa* eyes. It didn't matter which path I took through the store, they watched. And I made the mistake of telling the Pumpkin the children freaked me out. He took the news and ran with it.

The Pumpkin works at the store with me most Saturdays. He has a nine-to-five job. He tells his

Monday-through-Friday coworkers that on Saturdays, he sits with an elderly friend. Yes, that would be me. He isn't really wrong, but let me tell you, he's no spring chicken either. And while I'm on the subject, trust me, he's no Boy Scout.

We have store closing down to a science. We're motivated. It's time for dinner and a beverage or two. Skipping down the street, we go. Later, we would return. He drove to his home, and I went inside mine. Without me knowing, he'd moved the wooden children. I turned the corner, and there they were. I screamed every time. It was dark, the store was closed, and my brain moved too slowly to register that they weren't real.

Several times, he said something casual on the way home like "I don't remember locking the back door. Check it."

I would.

And there they were. Waiting on me. Just imagine the twins from *The Shining.* No doubt the Pumpkin was laughing the whole way home. Plotting where to move the creepy children next.

Shockingly, a customer purchased the girl, and that left the boy alone. Somehow, he was even scarier by himself. I wish I could tell you what eventually happened to him, but I can't. One day, he was there, the next, he was gone. He disappeared. I still look over my shoulder for him at Christmas, because I'm pretty sure the Pumpkin purchased the boy, and he's biding his time. Waiting for me to let my guard down. One day, when I least expect it, Easter, maybe, that boy will show up.

MAIN×24

MAINx24 is the most magical day of the year. A day filled with super-sparkly fun on the Southside.

What is MAINx24? It's a twenty-four-hour festival held on the first Saturday of December to celebrate the Southside. MAINx24 started in 2007, the brainchild of CreateHere, a neighborhood nonprofit. Today it's completely owned, organized, executed, and adored by the residents, merchants, and friends of the Southside community. It's a party. A huge block party that lasts all day and all night.

MAINx24 kicks off with a pancake breakfast at the fire department followed by a fabulous parade attracting tens of thousands and goes on to feature music, poetry, art, a chili cookoff, an adult Big Wheel race, activities for kids of all ages, Santa, Santa's entourage, boozy coffee, boozy food, and straight-up booze, jazz, a pooch parade, ballroom dancing, a dunk tank, chess, a light-your-bike ride, more people, more kids, more pets, more music, more food, and more booze.

This goes on for twenty-four perfectly scheduled hours packed with more than a hundred events. Every restaurant is filled to capacity, every small business slammed with wall-to-wall shoppers, and there's a smile on every face, including the hundreds upon hundreds of faces that pass through Merchants on Main. I was a MAINx24 spectator the first few years because our store hadn't opened yet, but even then, and to this day, I embrace it like my first glass of wine at happy hour. MAINx24 is not to be missed.

It was a few years after our store opened that my friend Mims and I were watching the parade with starry eyes when something clicked. We realized we were missing half the fun. "A float, Mims," I said. "We need a float." And the rest is history.

Her husband put a float team together and went to work. He located a flatbed trailer and built safety side rails, which, at the time, I didn't realize we needed, but he knew better than me, because the adult beverages started flowing early in the day. Too, there's the occasional sharp turn, slamming of the brakes, or pothole. There might even be a bar on our float. And in the middle of our float, there sits a gold throne.

Guess whose throne it is. Just guess.

You can't imagine the fun we've had with the float. We deck it out with anything that glitters, shines, or sparkles. The more, the better. Our float has miles of garland, snowflakes, wreaths, flamingos in their holiday attire, and anything we can get our hands on that screams, "*Celebrate!*" Every year, we think we've outdone ourselves, that our float couldn't be more festive or hold one more drop of decoration, only to outdo ourselves again the next year.

From our float, we toss Hershey's Kisses straight from Hershey, Pennsylvania, along with red, green, and silver Mardi Gras beads and small stuffed animals to the children in the crowd. The crowd tosses back Holly Jolly fireball Jell-O shots.

We call ourselves the Vixens. We wear sparkly boots and dance to everything from the B-52s' "Love Shack" to Queen's "We Are the Champions" to Lizzo's "Good as Hell." Everyone, and I mean everyone, along the parade route dances with us. I have no idea how long the parade actually lasts because we're so busy giving and receiving glittery love that it's always a shock when we reach the end. Trust me when I say we'd happily loop back through just to do it one more time.

It's truly the most wonderful day of the year, rain, snow, or shine, and we've paraded through it all. In the days leading up to the parade, we watch the weather on pins and needles. Like fourth and goal in overtime. Like election returns when no one has any idea which way Florida will go.

One year, the chances of rain wouldn't leave the forecast. In fact, they doubled down. It was almost a certainty that we'd be parading down Main Street in freezing rain. Could we possibly put a temporary tent over the float? How would that work? Was there such a thing as industrial Saran Wrap? We needed to see out, and the parade-goers needed to see the super-sparkly outfits we'd been working on since the Fourth of July.

We decided on clear bubble umbrellas, like the Queen of England carries during the rainy season, with clear plastic ponchos to cover our glittery parade wear. One of our Vixens, Dammit Janet, hit every CVS and Walgreens in Hamilton County. Disaster averted. Mission accomplished. And the forecast was right. It poured buckets. But by some miracle, not during the parade. Before and after, it was a washout. But during, we caught a break. Thank you, Parade Gods.

One year we'll never forget, it snowed. Sorta.

Along the route, we paused, slowing parade traffic for dramatic effect before the largest and most congregated crowd of parade watchers, in front of the fire hall. We got everyone's attention when we blasted "Uptown Funk" by Bruno Mars. And then, givers of magic and ambassadors of love that we are, we made it snow. We blasted snow into the air. Sparkly glittery snow, of course. It was, for one and all, a Christmas miracle. Snow. On a Southern day so warm and bright we probably needed sunscreen, we made it rain. I mean snow. We made it snow.

What's next? Bubble machines? T-shirt cannons? Glitter guns? A double-decker float with a mini marching band upstairs? Maybe next year, we'll be Rockettes. Because if anyone could pull it off, it's us. We start planning for the next parade as soon as we pull into the parking lot from the parade before. Any crazy, fun idea could become the next year's addition. How do you think the gold throne happened? A crazy, fun idea we saw through to a crazy fun reality.

After the parade, sober or not, we open the store. Usually to a line of customers. Half are waiting to shop. The other half are waiting to use our restroom, and you know what that means—my inevitable bathroom chores. The line to use our restroom during MAINx24 wasn't manageable ten years ago, and it certainly isn't today, so for the past several years, we've made the Porta Potty call. Remember the kid who tried to flush a whole roll of toilet paper? That was on a super-sparkly MAINx24 day. The line to the restroom was out the front door when his mother approached me.

Her: "Excuse me. There's something wrong with your toilet."

Me, just off the parade route, wearing a glitter crown, a cute dress in the shape of a Christmas tree, sparkly tights, and green glitter boots: "What?"

Her: "My son is hard on toilets."

Me, juggling the front desk, ringing up sales with sheets of gift wrap swirling around my head, the phone ringing off the hook, stocking stuffers being hurled at me from all directions: "Excuse me?"

Her: "He's hard on car doors too."

Me: "Did your son break the toilet?"

Her: "Maybe."

Me: "Ma'am, as you can see, we're very busy. Did your son break the toilet?"

Her: "Yes."

I did my very best, decked out in a Christmas tree dress and wearing green glitter boots, but in the end, it was a Porta Potty day for one and all.

Thanks a lot, kid.

Does this go on for twenty-four hours? It does

not. My patience, customer service, and plumbing skills wouldn't last that long. We are wonderfully crazy busy for as long as we are open, but at some point in the afternoon, things slow down. By then, we've had more new customers through the door than any other day of the year, we've said hello to all our favorite customers who've popped in just to say hi, and we've said, "Thank you!" to hundreds who stopped by to tell us they loved our float. When I look up and see more cocktails flowing than credit card swipes, I know it's time for last call before people start passing out, or God forbid, we lose the toilet for good, or someone with a badge asks to see my liquor license. (Something I don't have.)

If you think we lock the door, fall against it in relief, change out of our glittery attire, and find somewhere to curl up and take a nap, you don't know us at all. We lock up and hit the Southside. All it takes is a little more makeup, a squirt or two of hairspray, and a few more sparkles.

From its humble beginnings, MAINx24 has grown into a day that brings thousands to the Southside. A beautiful diverse crown of humanity that, along with us, has come to know and love the first Saturday in December. It's the brightest and most sparkly day of the year and does more for the prosperity and goodwill in our little corner of the world than anyone could ever imagine. It gives the term "shop small" an entirely new meaning. That day, it's "shop small, love big." The day is a gift. A gift we cherish. Along with every beating heart that joins the party.

See you next year at MAINx24! Or any day until then at Merchants on Main!

darling just believe
in yourself

I GET BY WITH A LITTLE HELP FROM MY FAVORITE QUOTES

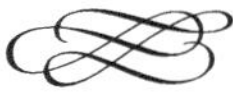

"Don't wait until you've reached your goal to be proud of yourself. Be proud of every step you take." ~Anonymous

"God didn't add another day in your life because you need it. He added it because someone out there needed you." ~Unknown

"She woke up every morning with the option of being anyone she wished. How beautiful it was that she always chose herself." ~Tyler Kent White

"I don't understand your specific kind of crazy, but I do admire your total commitment to it." ~Unknown

"She was beautiful but not like those girls in magazines. She was beautiful for the way she thought. She was beautiful for the sparkle in her eyes when she talked about something she loved. She was beautiful for her ability to make other people smile, even if she was sad. No, she wasn't beautiful for something as temporary as her looks. She was beautiful, deep down to her soul." ~F. Scott Fitzgerald

"Don't give up now. Chances are, your best kiss, your hardest laugh, and your greatest days are still yet to come." ~Atticus

"You keep putting one foot in front of the other, and then one day you look back, and you've climbed a mountain." ~Tom Hiddleston

"And one day, the girl with the books became the woman writing them." ~Kristen Costello

"You've always had the power, my dear. You just had to learn it for yourself." ~Glinda the Good Witch

"It was her habit to build up laughter out of inadequate materials." ~John Steinbeck, from *The Grapes of Wrath*

"If everything around you seems dark, look again. You may be the light." ~Rumi

"If the version of you from five years ago could see you right now, they'd be so proud. Keep going." ~Anonymous

"The butterfly is only beautiful because the caterpillar was brave." ~Anonymous

"God pulled you out of the pit so you could go

back in and get more people out. Never forget that." ~Adapted from Psalms 40:2

"Pour yourself a drink, put on some lipstick, and pull yourself together." ~Elizabeth Taylor

"Every storm runs out of rain." ~Maya Angelou

"My wish for you is that you continue. Continue to be who and how you are, to astonish a mean world with your acts of kindness. Continue to allow humor to lighten the burden of your tender heart." ~Maya Angelou

"It was only a sunny smile, and little it cost in the giving, but like morning light, it scattered the night and made the day worth living." ~F. Scott Fitzgerald.

thankful

FROM THE BOTTOM OF MY HEART

THROUGH THE YEARS, I'VE WRITTEN SEVERAL CHAPTERS of my story, jotting down short thoughts about the funny things that happen at the store. It was during Covid lockdown, the pandemic, the quarantine of 2020 when the world closed, and I had so much time on my hands that I had no choice but to finish telling my story. I moved forward with what would be this book.

All the restaurants on the Southside closed. I had to feed myself. (Horrors.) A few had takeout service, but takeout is like feeding myself—too quiet—and I'm a people person. I missed my regular customers, of course, but oddly, I found myself missing the crazy ones too. The pageantry of crazy that never stopped walking through my door.

I dressed and went downstairs every day to work in the store. Some days, I even wore makeup. Other days, yoga pants. And speaking of yoga, Zoom yoga saved my somewhat shaky sanity.

Often, the phone rang with customers checking on me, and I'll be forever grateful for their kindness. To hear their voices was a gift. There were times the phone rang and the wonderful voice on the other end would ask to buy puzzles, a baby gift, or a gift card. I did curb service, gifts wrapped and ready to go, retail takeout. The worst were the truly quiet days. Those days, I became Crazy Orchid Lady. I named and labeled all forty or more of my orchids. (They weren't all expressly mine. Some were rescues my friends tried to kill.) Yes, I talked to them. Don't judge me.

During lockdown, while the store was closed, I appreciated my friends and extended family more than ever before. I missed smiles. I missed hugs. I missed my neighbors. I missed my trivia, bingo, brunch, and wine-time friends to a level I didn't know possible. None of us could have imagined the isolation, the introspection, and the good and bad that would come from almost solitary confinement. For me? This book. And it would never have happened without my family and friends. How can I say thank-you enough? I've been given a gift I can never repay.

Thank you to the Southside neighborhood that embraced me and my daughter. Lifting us up with laughter and friendship. You made the bad days bearable with the smallest of kindnesses.

Thank you to all my adopted children and fabulous friends of the bartender, server, Danimal, and Feed corner table varieties. Your generous pours, favorite songs, laughter, encouragement, and kindness turned so many of my days around. Ian, you are missed.

Thank you to my amazing dealers at Merchants on Main who stayed with me through the worst days of the storm, when most would have jumped from what felt like a sinking ship.

Thank you, Covid Boyfriend. A man with a beautiful heart and a scary-smart math brain. (He's really cute too.)

Thank you, Kevin's mom. Beautiful Book Fairy. You reminded me to believe in miracles and brought so much joy into my world. With your magic wand, you've made my dreams come true. These have been some of my happiest days, writing with your help and encouragement.

Thank you to my partners in crime, my MAINx24 parade vixens. Strong, gorgeous, and sparkly women who make the best day of the year even better!

From the bottom of my heart, thank you to my

adopted son, the Pumpkin. There is no better gift on this earth than that of laughing with you. From the first moments on the crazy train I found myself on, you were there. You are loved.

Thank you to Sweet Angel Child from Heaven. My beautiful, brave, badass daughter. You've weathered every storm with me and helped create our new world. I'm so proud of you for so many reasons. You are a gift. You are loved beyond words.

With love all the way to the liquor store and back,

Missy Steiner

ABOUT THE AUTHOR

Missy Steiner is a native of Chattanooga, Tennessee. Her store is a fixture on the Southside. It's from her perch at the register, ringing up customers, where most of the crazy unfolds. Visit her there anytime and follow Merchants on Main on Facebook and Instagram.

PAPERPRODUCTS DESIGN
PAPERPRODUCTS DESIGN
LOVE
YOU

Made in United States
Orlando, FL
08 November 2022

24348577R00109